Comprehensive Guide to Mastering Animation Techniques

Yasser .Y Velasquez

Funny helpful tips:

Engage with books that explore art; they offer a window into human expression and cultural evolution.

Harness the potential of smart homes; automated systems are enhancing comfort, security, and energy efficiency.

*Comprehensive Guide to Mastering Animation Techniques :
The Ultimate Step-by-Step Guide to Stunningly Creative
Animation Techniques: Boost Your Skills and Unleash Your
Imagination.*

<u>Life advices:</u>

Stay committed to quality; it builds brand reputation and customer loyalty.

Engage with the world of smart contracts; they automate and verify contractual processes on blockchain platforms.

Introduction

Embark on a transformative journey through the world of animation mastery. This guide is your compass, steering you towards the pinnacle of animator expertise.

It all begins with a warm greeting, acknowledging your ambitions. Along the way, you'll encounter some truths that set the stage for your growth. These insights form the foundation for your path forward.

Your plan takes shape, guiding you through crucial initial steps. You'll explore the diverse spectrum of animation and learn how to set and pursue your goals effectively.

However, mastering animation isn't just about technical skills. Essential mental skills become your allies, helping you navigate distractions, stay focused, and manage time efficiently.

The importance of critique becomes evident, offering you a pathway for improvement. Mentorship and external resources play a pivotal role in your development, guiding you towards well-rounded skills.

From honing visualization to grasping basic principles, you'll delve into the core of animation creation. Your journey through computer skills and hands-on tools ensures you're equipped with the necessary expertise.

Practice becomes your constant companion, evolving your animation abilities. With exercises covering various aspects, you'll refine your craft step by step.

Your venture into the animation industry extends to crafting an effective demo reel and portfolio. Through this, you'll learn to present your abilities and stand out in the competitive field.

In the end, you'll summarize your voyage, armed with the vital lessons you've gathered. You'll understand yourself, how to learn effectively, and the essential skills you need. Avoiding pitfalls and understanding the job market complete your preparation.

This guide is your ticket to animation mastery, paving the way for you to become an exceptional animator.

Contents

CHAPTER ONE: Series
Introduction

What These Books Are About

An education in animation is a never ending pursuit of excellence. There is no end to the road; no point at which you can stop learning and say, "That's it, I know everything now." From its crude beginnings, animation as an art form has evolved aesthetically and technically into the marvel that it is today. This has been accomplished by talented and ambitious individuals that looked at the state of the art and asked, "Where can we go from here?" In order to become one of these animation pioneers, you will first need to learn as much as you can about the current state of animation techniques.

Obviously, one must start with the basics and there are plenty of resources for that – other books, schools, courses and the internet. But what then? Normally, advanced technical knowledge can only be gained through years of experience. Working in small Jack-of-all-trades studios and large studios with highly experienced animators that are willing to teach is a fantastic way to develop the skills that an animator requires to excel. The problem is that studios are not schools – they are jobs. If you have been hired by a studio, they expect you to know what you are doing, and rightly so! You couldn't expect to get a job in a hospital as a surgeon without knowing what you are doing and expect the other doctors to teach you what you are supposed to already know.

These books should help to bridge that gap. They will give you not only a set of advanced tools and techniques to speed you on your way but also a way of thinking differently—a way of seeing, feeling and studying the world around you that will enable you to learn on your own much faster than ever before.

You will learn how to act through your characters effortlessly and without stereotypes or clichés. The world will become your classroom and you will know how to study and store information from the people and things that you see every day and how to use them in your work. By learning some basic physics and methods for internalizing actions, you will be able to go far beyond moving lines on paper or joints on a screen. This series also attempts to break many long standing myths and bad habits that have plagued animators over the years. Through technical information and practical exercises, you will learn how to improve your acting skills, develop character building skills and start building a library of personality traits.

Beyond technical skills, these books will also help you to understand what kind of animator you are and what kind of studio or work situation you need to thrive. The How To Animate series is for people that have already learned the basics of animation and are ready to move on. If you are a traditional or stop motion animator, there are books in this series that can help you to make the transition to 3D. If you learned how to animate on a computer, the information in these pages can help you develop the necessary skills to animate in any medium.

There is a lot more to being an animator than just knowing how to animate. Whether you are working in a big studio, a small studio or a home studio, you will still be faced with many of the same problems – deadlines, artist's block, dealing with egos (yours and other people's), studio politics and much more. Learning to survive the lifestyle is a skill that you will learn over many years but it doesn't have to be all hard knocks. These books will help point out some of the pitfalls and obstacles that you are likely to face throughout your career. Armed with this knowledge, you stand a better chance of enjoying every moment of your chosen career.

What These Books Are NOT About

This is not a series about the basics of animation. You won't find any bouncing balls, walk cycles, basic drawing lessons, animation history, summary of the 12 principles or any of the other fundamentals that you will find in other books. If you don't already have a basic understanding of how animation is created, it would be wise to learn it before trying to absorb the information in this book. The two books that every animator should own are "The Animator's Survival Kit" by Richard Williams and "Disney Animation - The Illusion of Life" by Frank Thomas and Ollie Johnston. Both of these books are vast – the fundamentals are not simple...

Although these books cover animation principles for many animation mediums, they do not contain any specifics about the basic functions of any software packages. If you need to choose a software package to purchase, this first book may help you decide which would suit you best. However, it won't teach you which buttons to push. For every 3D animation program available, there are several books, videos, DVD's and online tutorials that will teach you everything you need to know about how to use them properly. This series of books will teach you the skills you need to bring your characters to life within those programs (or on paper, in clay, sand, machine parts or whatever).

CHAPTER TWO:
Introduction

Hello Animators!

What you're about to read is the first of 26 books on animation that I have been writing for over 18 years. This series, <u>How To Animate</u> is a collection of everything I have learned so far in my 30+ year career. This book, "Advancing Your Animation Beyond The Basics" is actually the last book that I conceived—it's the gateway to all the others. It will show you what skills you need to learn to become a great animator. The other books in this series will teach you those skills. Obviously, my books are not the only information out there, so I will also help guide you to other sources of information that will speed you on your way.

This book will teach you how to become a great animator without having to spend tens of thousands of dollars going to school. By the end of the book, you will have a solid plan for success, including a description of the wide variety of skills you need to learn and how to find the resources to learn it all as inexpensively as possible.

We will cover ways of discovering your own personalized method of learning, daily training techniques, and how to fast-track your learning to cut years off of your training time.

This series is <u>not</u> an introduction to animation—it is not intended for people that have no clue about the animation process at all. There are quite a few really good books out there that will get you started and you can find a list of them on my website at <u>www.howtoanimate.net</u>. <u>How To Animate</u> is for animators at all stages of their development that are ready to train themselves to become great animators.

This book and the ones to follow may not be the thickest books in your library, but not because they lack information. There is no fluff here to pad out the pages and no "history of animation" or other subjects that have already been covered a thousand times in other books.

Your time is valuable and I respect that. You want the info and you want it quickly, in a way that you can absorb it and use it immediately. I'm the same as you—I buy a ton of Kindle books and as I read them, I'm constantly checking my progress to see how much longer it's going to take to get through it. If it's taken a lot of reading, yet I'm only a fraction of the way through the book and I feel that I haven't learned much of value yet, there's a very real chance that I will stop reading and never return to it.

My plan is to be as concise as possible so I can pack as much useful info into as small a space as possible. For the most part, you should be able to get through each of these books in a single sitting. I have a summary at the end of the book that may save you from having to take a lot of notes.

I have decided to keep the illustrations to a minimum—to use them only when necessary to illustrate a point. I have lots of books that are filled with great pictures that I have never actually read through fully because the pictures and captions were too much of a distraction—the words just didn't seem as important or interesting. I plan to stuff your head with knowledge, not fill your eyes with pretty pictures.

The series is broken into 3 groups of books and I recommend that you read them in order—if you try and jump ahead, there will be terms and techniques used that you won't understand yet.

Group 1 will teach you all of the basic and advanced techniques and skills you will use every day, from physics to acting, to higher concepts like texture and composition.

Group 2 teaches specific challenges, like animals, villains and children. You will need to use all of the tools that you learned in group 1 to use these books successfully.

Group 3 takes you into the real world and teaches you how to survive in various work situations, such as big studios, surviving as a freelancer and as a brand new animator.

A Bit About Me

Before you commit yourself to reading a series of 26 books, you're probably going to want to see my credentials... My name is Chris Derochie and I've been in animation since 1984.

I've worked at studios of all sizes, such as Don Bluth Studios and Disney (the Australian Branch); I've done traditional animation, 3d, visual effects, features, tv and games. I've worked on projects of all sizes and styles, from A Goofy Movie to District 9 to small game projects. I ran my own service studio in Ireland for 10 years as well.

I have taught animation for many years in schools around the world and I've been an animation supervisor for over 15 years.

...and I never spent a day in school learning any of it.

When I started learning animation, the resources for learning on your own were pretty minimal—there were some books on the basics and if you were lucky, you might be able to learn from someone that was willing to mentor you. Otherwise, you had to go to school or just try to figure it all out for yourself with trial and error. There was no such thing as the internet at the time, which was unfortunate—the internet is about to become your best friend!

Alright, time to take your first step!

CHAPTER THREE: Some
Hard Truths

Just So We're Clear...

Please don't think that I'm saying in my introduction that schools are bad and that you shouldn't go there. School may be just what you need—all I'm saying is that it's not the only way to learn, nor is it necessarily the fastest and it certainly isn't the cheapest way... Some people need the discipline of a school system to keep them motivated. Some people need to be around other students—to learn from them and to keep themselves happy. However, there are two comments I have heard again and again from animators that spent years in school: "It wasn't worth the money" and "I wish someone had taught me that in school..." (usually after I explained some aspect of physics or acting).

Remember, even if school is the right path for you, some schools are better than others and cost is not an indication of quality. You need to do your homework and really investigate the schools you're interested in. Read reviews, talk to people and get recommendations. If you don't, you could be making a very costly mistake!

One thing that you need to have as you study animation is feedback! You must have someone that knows what they are talking about critique your work. Not only to tell you what you have done wrong but also to point out what you did right (which may have been accidental!) so you will be able to repeat that success again in the future. You can't progress in a vacuum, you need critique.

In the end, the true value of a school is the quality of the feedback that you get. I've heard about schools that have terrible teachers that give little to no feedback—the students learn by teaching each other, but that's the blind leading the blind... Yes, it's great to get feedback from your fellow students but they usually have zero experience and aren't qualified as teachers either. They may be able to tell you if something looks bad or if it looks good but they probably won't be able to tell you <u>why</u> or how to fix it if it's not working. If you're going to learn on your own, you need to find a mentor. If you're going to go to school, choose the one with the best teachers. You will need to read reviews and talk to people that went to those schools recently. Keep in mind, just because a school got bad reviews 10 years ago, does not mean that it is still a bad place to go—it may have been revamped, the bad teachers may be gone, leaving much better ones in their place.

One bad review doesn't make a bad school. Remember that everyone that goes to the school will have their own individual experience there— someone may have hated it there for very valid reasons, while someone else loved it for the very same reasons. If several people complain about the same shortcomings, and those reviews are recent, that's when you have to consider striking that school off your list.

Some Hard Truths

If you decide that the school path is for you, it could be ridiculously expensive! When I was doing my research for this book, I looked into the cost of several popular schools and I was shocked to see how quickly the costs have been rising—one school had raised their price by $10,000 <u>per course</u> in the past 2 years! I have seen tuition fees range from as low as $11,000 to as high as $84,000 per year. You'll have to do your own research into the costs, just remember to factor in ALL the costs—tuition, accommodation, fees and any books, equipment and materials you will need. No matter how you look at it, it's a hefty price tag that you will probably be paying off for many years to come.

The common thinking among animation students is that you have to go to school to learn animation and that you won't get a job unless you went to a really good school. While it may be true that the HR department in many studios have a relationship with certain schools, I have never seen a studio in which the decision to hire an animator is made by the HR department... The decision maker is always a lead artist or supervisor. They really don't give a hoot what school you went to and I can guarantee that they have absolutely zero interest in what your grades were. They are only interested in three things:

1. **Your demo reel** - if the quality of your work is high and it's the kind of work that they are currently in need of, you will probably get hired.

2. **Your experience** - if your work is great, a lack of experience isn't necessarily a deal breaker. Having some experience is always a plus, though.

3. **Are you going to fit in or are you a jerk** - this is what the interview is for; to find out what your personality is like. If you won't fit in, it doesn't matter how good your work is, you probably won't get hired.

So, if a degree means nothing to most animation studios, why is it thought to be so important? Well, if you plan to work in a different country and you're not a citizen or resident, a degree can get you on the legal fast track. Studios (especially the ones in places with government tax incentives) will hire foreigners with degrees over ones without degrees because it saves them weeks of time and effort and a lot of expense. However (and this is really important!) it does NOT have to be a degree in <u>animation!</u> It can be a degree in anything! Yes, a degree in basket weaving or floor sweeping (if there was such a thing) will still qualify you for that legal fast track. So, if you need a degree, find the cheapest, fastest one you can get—don't get yourself in debt for life just to get an animation degree when it really has no real world value.

Laws change, so pay attention to what the current situation is when you decide to look for a job in another country. For example, as I was making the final preparations to publish this book, the laws in Canada changed drastically! Foreign animators no longer qualify for the tax credits, so they are much more expensive to employ than citizens or people with permanent resident status. There are several other restrictions that have been introduced that make it nearly impossible for studios in Canada to hire foreign workers within their budgets. Before you make any plans to work in another country, get some professional advice!

If your main reason for going to school is just to get a degree, then you need to be sure that degree has any value to you at all. The main reason that most people go to school for animation (and this isn't too much of a stretch) is to learn animation. Obvious, right? However, as I explained earlier, not every school will do a good job at teaching you animation and the feedback you get might be close to useless. If you feel like you have the drive and discipline to learn on your own, then keep reading—I'm about to teach you how to do it.

As for the cost, if you're reading this for free on my website, then smile inwardly at this fact—all of the rest of the books in this series will be free to read online as well. The advertising on the site helps offset my costs and it would be great if you could donate some money if these books help launch your career. If you want to take the book around with you as a kindle book or an actual printed copy, there is a cost to that, but they will always be free to read on the website.

CHAPTER FOUR:
Planning Your Path

The field of study for animation is big—really, really big! If you want to be a great animator, you need to focus squarely on animation—don't get distracted by modelling or rigging or any other field. Almost every generalist I've ever known says that their weakest skill is animation... That's because it takes more time and effort to learn animation than all their other skills combined.

Even if you're just learning animation, it's still too vast a subject to learn without specializing. It's kind of like saying "I want to learn to be an engineer". What kind of engineering? You can't easily learn to be a civil engineer, a chemical engineer and a mechanical engineer, let alone try to learn all the different types of engineering at the same time... Same thing with animation—figure out what you want to specialize in and focus on learning it to the best of your ability, then you can branch out from there.

For example, I started off in traditional animation over 30 years ago and I specialized in human characters. I eventually got better at more cartoony characters, but it took time. 15 years into my career, I started learning 3d animation. I later added Visual Effects animation—creatures, hard surface (vehicles and spaceships) and digidoubles (realistic human replacements). Even now, 30 years later, I'm still not great at crazy, stylized 2d characters because I never really studied that style and I didn't have a natural skill for that way of thinking.

When I worked on the Aladdin sequels and tv show, I used to hand off my parrot and genie animation to Steve Taylor—he was far better at that style than I was—and in exchange, I would take his Aladdin and Jasmine scenes. By working our strengths, we were both able to get through more shots and we learned a lot from each other. Still, I will never be as good at that style of animation as someone like Eric Goldberg or Murray Debus because I haven't dedicated all of my focus to that line of study, like I would have to do to become a master.

Make sure you're sitting down for this next part—it tends to shock a lot of people...

When I worked at Don Bluth Studios, John Pomeroy gave a lecture that I will never forget. Well, to be honest, I've forgotten a lot of it—mostly because one of his opening remarks shocked me so much that I didn't hear a lot of what came afterwards... What he said was, "When you're first starting out in animation, you know, for your first 10 years or so, you're in the beginner phase." He went on to describe how in that beginner phase, everything is a struggle as you learn the craft. After you master the basics and the process becomes more second nature, you can focus solely on the acting.

I have to admit, my brain melted at that point. I hadn't realized that mastering animation was so lengthy a process that you were still considered a beginner when you had 10 years of experience! What I have discovered since then is that 10 years is an average. I have worked with animators that were amazing after 6 or 7 years. I have also worked with quite a few that were still pretty terrible after 25 years... You're probably thinking that it's all about talent. Well, it's actually not. It really depends on the amount of deliberate practice you put in. What I mean by that is that you need to have a good plan for how you are going to learn and improve and you have to make actual, concentrated effort to achieve those goals on a regular basis—every day, if possible.

It has been theorized that in order to master any skill, you need to put in 10,000 hours of deliberate practice. Although this is a generalization and not necessarily true in all cases, it's still a good benchmark. To restate that, if you were really determined to master animation as fast as possible, (using the 10,000 hour benchmark) you would have to practice for 8 hours a day, 7 days a week for almost 3 1/2 years! So, 10 years of more sensible hours doesn't sound all that far fetched, does it? Of course, that still takes dedication! To put it into very realistic terms, if you studied and practiced for only 2 hours a day, 5 days a week <u>without fail</u>, then it would take you <u>19.2 years</u> to master that skill... You don't want this to take forever, so you need to spend as much time as possible dedicating yourself to animation.

Keep in mind, I'm talking about mastering one speciality of animation, not mastering all there is to know about animation—no one can live long enough to do that...

Alright—so we know that the start of this journey has a lot of paths to choose from—how do you make an informed decision about which path to choose? If you're about to spend years of effort trying to follow this path, you'd better be sure you've picked the one that's right for you!

How do you do that?!?

The best way that I know of to find your path is to learn more about yourself so you can find out what will make you truly happy. As "airy-fairy" as that sounds, there is a process you can follow to hone in on it.

First of all, don't just latch on to "popular" dreams, such as "I want to work for Pixar" or "I want to make my own film". When you learn about who you really are, what makes you tick and what you're really passionate about, you may discover that some of those popular dreams don't really suit you at all!

Your First Steps

There are 2 very important questions that you need to ask yourself:

      1. What is my passion?

      2. What is my animation "mindset"?

Let's start with passion. Why is it important to know? Most people try to answer this question with a very basic, "surface level" answer of, "I'm passionate about animation" but you need to go a lot deeper than that and here's why—some day, you are going to be in a job or situation where nothing is going right and everything is painful. You'll be there, sitting at your desk, hating your life and wondering why you got into this crazy business in the first place. Some people can get overwhelmed by this and they quit the industry altogether, thinking that it's just not worth it or that they aren't cut out for it. Other people can get very jaded—they keep working but they lose all the fun and it becomes just another job—a way of making money.

If you find yourself in this kind of dark place, stop and ask yourself this question, "What did I get into this business for in the first place? What is it that I'm so passionate about that will make this all worthwhile? Am I in the right place to feed that passion...?"

Now, as you can see, if you don't have a clue what you're passionate about, how are you going to know if your current job is servicing your needs?

You need to ask yourself what excites and interests you about animation, then for each answer you give yourself, ask again about that aspect. Keep peeling away the layers until you get to the core of what you love. Once you hit that, you'll realize that there are lots of things you can do to service that basic need—that fire at the heart of everything you do.

As an example, let me take you through the process I went through a long time ago.

For a long time, my dream had been to make my own animated features. I wanted to make them in a way that no one had ever done before. I had a solid vision for what I wanted them to look and feel like. I knew what kind of stories I wanted to tell and I had a plan for achieving it.

One day, I was in the back yard of my house in Ireland, raking up the moss (there's a lot of that in Ireland...) so I had several uninterrupted hours to think. I was quite unhappy with how my career was going and I wasn't sure why. I had my own studio that I had been running for a few years and I had already had a good career as an animator. I was working towards my goals, so why was it feeling so hollow?

Luckily, I asked myself that important question, "What happened to all that passion I used to have for animation? Why did I get into this business in the first place?!?"

It's important to note that animation wasn't always my dream—I originally wanted to be a comic book artist. I kind of fell into animation accidentally and stuck with it after I discovered that I had a talent for it. That was my first clue that my passion wasn't wrapped up solely in animation.

First, I focused my questions on animation. "Is it drawing that I love the most? Since I'm doing mostly 3d now, am I unhappy because I'm not drawing?" As I thought about it, I realized that I loved drawing comic book styled characters and realism, but I was less interested in animation style drawing, so it wasn't a common thread.

"Is it the animation lifestyle that I love the most? Would I do this for free just to be able to do this everyday alongside other artists and be part of that community?"

Nope. If I wasn't being paid for it, I wouldn't do it. Also, I really enjoyed working from home as much or more than working in a studio.

"Is it the process? Do I love the whole method of making a film or tv show?" No. If that was the case, I would love every project I worked on and clearly, some were more fun than others.

I realized that I had to start getting more specific with my questions. In order to do that, I needed to find the common thread in the things that I loved doing. I had wanted to be a comic book artist, I loved animation, I also loved writing, reading books, watching movies, entertaining kids, acting and painting. What could possibly be the common thread to all of that?!?

Acting seemed to be a common thread. (A little weak in some respects, like reading and painting) but when I asked myself if it was acting, I found a way to get deeper. I said, "If all I was allowed to do was act, would I be happy?" It was getting closer, but it still wasn't right.

Then I decided to peel away another layer. "What is it about acting that I loved?" I hated being watched and judged but there was something about performing that thrilled me. Maybe that's why I preferred acting while hidden behind a character... Did that explain the comic book passion?

Sort of.

It still didn't explain the painting, drawing or reading, though.

Acting (with or without my body) involved performance, storytelling, eliciting an emotional response in an audience, feeling and projecting emotion and communicating with other people. Were any of those aspects applicable to my other interests?

Then it hit me!

Stories!

Why did I love reading?—The stories grab me and pull me in. My visualization skills are very good, so a good story allows me to see and experience an entire world as if I was there.

Why did I love comics?—Again, it was the stories that I was passionate about. I hated stories that were shallow or simply about a fight between a good guy and a bad guy. I loved rich, deep, character driven stories that weren't easy to predict.

Painting?—Yup! With the style of painting I liked, it was like telling a story in a single image.

Acting? Entertaining kids? Writing?—Of course! Story was the common thread I had been looking for!

What about making my own films? Why did that become such a strong goal?—I realized that it was because I had stories to tell—lots of them! I wanted to tell my stories my own way. That was why I wanted to make comics, why I wanted to make films and why I loved writing! It also explained why I wasn't as interested in making other people's films—they weren't my stories.

Then I asked that all important question...

"If all I was able to do was tell and read stories, would I be happy?" The answer, at last, was a resounding YES!!!!

I realized that there were other paths open to me—I could be a novelist, an actor, or any other job or activity that involved storytelling and I would be happy because I would be doing something I was truly passionate about. That explained why so many of the jobs I had been doing with my own company had left me feeling so unfulfilled.

That knowledge has also helped me choose the right jobs and avoid ones that would drain the life out of me. For example, I found that I really enjoyed doing previs animation because I was able to have so much input into how the story was told—through the acting, cinematography and editing—I find it very fulfilling.

Keep in mind, that was _my_ passion that I found—yours may be very different. I know some people that love the process of drawing or working on the computer and they are happy as long as they get to do that. For some, they want to see their name up in lights, so seeking out the biggest and best films to work on is their path to happiness. For others, it's all about completion—they get the most satisfaction out of seeing a project get completed (those people tended to gravitate toward production in the end).

Take the time to figure this out now—you don't want to wait until you're decades down the wrong path, having spent years being unhappy without knowing why.

The Animation Spectrum

Now it's time for that other really important question—What is my animation mindset—my position on the "Animation Spectrum"? Yeah, I know—another confusing, ambiguous term... You probably haven't read about this in any books, I made up the term myself a long time ago. Of course, I'm going to help you understand it by telling you another old story. (Now you know why I use stories to explain everything...)

I discovered way back in 1991 that the way animators view what animation is all about can vary wildly. Think of it like a political spectrum, with a left wing and right wing as opposite points of view and a moderate center.

I was 24 years old and still naive enough to think that all animators thought and felt the same way that I did. I was working as an animator in Don Bluth Studios in Ireland at the time and was even more jazzed than usual on this particular day because we had a very special guest—Chuck Jones! He came for a tour of the studio and he was gracious enough to give us a Q&A session in our screening room afterward!

As the session wore on and people asked him questions about his life and career, I finally got my chance to speak and I asked the one question that I was dying to have answered. Thinking back to all that he had created and how much he had inspired a generation of people, not only animators, I asked him, "Where would you like to see animation go in the future?"

His response stunned me because it was so far out of line with my "animation world view".

(I wish that his exact words had been recorded, but this is as accurate as I can recall and I am paraphrasing...)

"There really isn't anything left to discover. Everything there is to know about animation is like a nugget in the ground—Disney's 9 Old Men have already uncovered it all. Animation is like the orchestra—there hasn't been an instrument invented for the orchestra in over 100 years. It's complete as it is. We simply use the instruments in different combinations to make new music."

When I recovered enough to speak, I said, "Well, why not invent new instruments?"

"It's already complete as it is" was his reply.

"But what was the last instrument invented?" I asked. (I think it was the piano...) What if they had never invented the piano. What if they had said, 'Well, we've got this harpsichord and all of these other instruments—that's it, the orchestra is complete!' Then we would never have had any of Beethoven's famous piano work or Rachmaninoff's famous piano concertos, (not to mention all the other music and genres that grew out of the existence of the piano). If someone hadn't invented the piano, we wouldn't even know that that kind of music could exist! Who knows what we've missed out on for the past 100 years because no one took the next step and invented a new instrument!"

He said that our job as animators was to use what we have and to mix it around to create new works, like writing symphonies by varying the instruments of the orchestra.

I told him that I thought our job was to push the boundaries and discover new things, new principles and techniques that have never been thought of before. Just like the people that wrote music before the piano had been invented, we don't even know what new things we will invent in the future and how it will change everything.

The conversation continued for quite a while and it eventually dawned on me that neither of us was right or wrong, we just had completely opposite points of view of what the nature of animation was. I looked forward to change and new development, while he drew comfort from the belief that the knowledge was complete already and he was free to do what he was comfortable with and what he knew so well—to create within those established boundaries.

The more that I thought about this and the more people I talked to about it, the more I realized that we all seemed to fit onto a scale. At one end—the far left, we have what I call the "Archaeologists"- people that think that the principles of animation are finite and have already been completely uncovered. On the far right, we have the "Pioneers"—people that believe that there is no limit to the knowledge of animation; that the principles have been invented, not discovered, and that they can continue to be developed indefinitely.

Every one of you falls somewhere on that scale.

"That's great", I hear you say, "so what?"

Here's the kicker... All studios also fall somewhere on this scale and it's important that you choose your jobs based on how well you align with the studio on the scale.

For example, very large studios tend to be Archaeological types. They have developed their formula over years and they have their own, repeatable, formulaic way of doing everything. If you are a pioneering type and you go to work in a place like that, prepare to be frustrated... You will want to be doing things in new ways or to try new things that you have never done before. If you have to do the same things every day in exactly the same way for too long, you're going to go NUTS! You will feel stifled, sidelined and stagnant.

Likewise, if you're an Archaeologist, you would hate to be in a pioneering studio, like many studios that do commercials, for example. Archaeologists love the safe, familiar feeling of going in to work each day knowing exactly what they are doing and feeling secure in the fact that they have the skills to do the job in the tradition that it has been done in for many years. In a pioneering studio, they would feel like they had the rug pulled out from under them! They would have to struggle every day to face new challenges—to do things they have never even thought about doing before and to find solutions to problems that they have never had to face. It would be scary and unnerving for them.

Now is it starting to make sense? If you discover that you are a really right winged pioneering type, do you think that a long term job in a big Archaeologist studio will be right for you? Just because it's a popular dream, doesn't mean that it's right for you.

One other important thing to consider—the mindset of a studio can change over time! It really depends on the people in charge. Disney is a perfect example. When Walt Disney was in charge, it was the most pioneering studio ever! They invented everything from concepts like the 12 principles, to techniques like the multi plane camera. After he was gone, the studio shifted and became much more of an Archaeologist's paradise. When you choose a studio, consider where they are on the scale at this moment and be ready to move on if the studio shifts away from what makes you happy.

Setting Goals

So, you know what you're really passionate about and you know exactly where you fall on the scale, so you feel confident and ready to go out and get your dream job, right? Hold on a sec, there's one more important thing to consider first to prevent you from steering off that path you've just found. Yeah, just like your parents may have taught you, you need to set some goals.

I'm not going to spend a lot of time on this because there are a lot of great sources out there to learn goal setting techniques. I'll get you started, then I urge you to carry on with someone more qualified to train you. The best goal setting training I've ever heard of is from life coach Tony Robbins. Go to tonyrobbins.com to learn more. No, I don't get any kickbacks from him —he doesn't even know I exist, but I have learned a ton of vital things from his courses.

So, why are goals so vitally important? Do you have a dream for yourself and your career? Dreams aren't goals—dreams are an end result that you want to achieve. A goal is a plan—it's how you are going to achieve that dream. Think of a goal as a dream with a timeline...

Let's say, for example, that your dream is to make your own feature someday. You may hold that dream close to your heart all your life but how will you feel when you wake up in 20 years and realize that you're no closer to achieving it than you were when you started; or worse, you've actually gone down the wrong path and now you're trapped, further away from your goal than when you began...

The way to make those dreams a reality is to set long-term, mid-term and short-term goals. Write them down and review them at least once a year to see if they are still relevant or if you need to revise or redefine them. Make a 1, 5, 10 and 20 year plan.

They need to be specific, actionable items—things you can actually take action and do. Be as specific as you can!

For example, if the dream is to make your own feature, there are many possibilities for a long-term goal to achieve it. It could be, "I want to start a studio with a small crew of highly talented people, to create my film my own way, to be sold later as a finished product."

Or it might be, "I want to create a fantastic concept for a film that I can sell to a studio with myself attached as the director."

Or maybe something like, "I want to make a film completely on my own and I don't care how many years it takes. I can sell it later or distribute it on the internet so the whole world can see it."

These are all very valid long-term goals for achieving the same dream—to make a feature film. Do you see how it's more specific, though? Can you see that there is a definite path of action that needs to be followed?

From there, you will come up with your mid-term goals. If your plan is to have a small group of talented artists and you want to be established and making these films in 20 years time, then by the 10-15 year mark, you had better have established a good relationship with a lot of great artists so they will trust you enough to get onboard with you and make a feature. That means you have to start making a dream team list of people right away and start trying to get to know them—work in the studios that they are working in; connect to them on LinkedIn and start having conversations with them etc.

If you want to make your films yourself, then a great mid-term goal would be to have all the technical knowledge you need to pull it off, so you're going to have to do a lot of studying and get a lot of practical experience. In the short-term, you're going to have to decide what the best and fastest way to learn would be. That may involve choosing the right school, finding the right free information or getting yourself a mentor or two.

Your short-term goals are the stepping stones that get you to the moon in little bite-sized chunks. Following on with our example, if you want to direct your own features, some good-short term goals might be to find out what the best books and courses on directing are. Picking the best of those books and reading it within a specific timeframe is also an effective short-term goal.

Keep this important distinction in mind—the difference between a dream and a goal is a time limit. If you don't set a schedule or time limit on your goals, they aren't really solid goals. You have to be able to track your progress.

Excellent! So, now you know what you're passionate about, you know your mindset AND you have a clear set of goals! You're ready to start learning and get on that path to glory! The really big question burning in your mind right now is probably, "What specific skills do I need to learn to become a great animator?"

But... before I can answer that, there's one last thing you need to figure out —how to learn! This really is something they should teach everyone in school...

CHAPTER FIVE:
Learning How to Learn

As I mentioned before, you're never going to be a master of everything in your lifetime, so you need to fast-track your knowledge and only learn what you need to know <u>right now</u> in order to progress. Try to resist the urge to learn everything right away and definitely avoid learning extraneous skills that aren't immediately helpful. You need to learn along a narrow path of what is essential and you need to do it in the most effective way for y<u>ou</u>.

In order to learn as fast as possible, you need to figure out how you learn the best. Everyone has their own individual way of learning and retaining knowledge—some methods that work really well for them and other ways that really <u>don't</u> work for them!

Do you learn best from reading things, like a text book or tutorial? Is video training better for you, like <u>Lynda.com</u> or Digital Tutors (now called Pluralsight)? Do you need hands-on experience and experimentation for the learning to sink in? Maybe it's a combination of all the above! Can you motivate yourself or do you need someone to kick your butt? Do you learn best on your own or do you need a classroom environment or a peer group? Perhaps one-on-one training with a mentor is the best method for you. Figure it out so you don't end up spinning your wheels.

Your Biggest Challenge

One of the greatest obstacles you will have to face is your own mental inhibitions. Like they say in sports, you have to win the mental game! You will question yourself, doubt your own ability to learn and probably feel like a complete fraud at times—most artists do, it's just part of the territory. Trust me, we all go through it. I've talked about this for many years and I always receive a lot of "wow, that sounds just like me" sort of reactions. I just recently discovered that this phenomenon is called Imposter Syndrome and it's a very common problem with high achieving people, especially perfectionists. Don't worry, it's not a mental illness or a personality trait, it's a reaction to certain stimulus. Google it and read about it for yourself—you're not alone!

It's not going to be easy to get past your fears and inhibitions—you just have to learn that they will never go away completely, you have to be courageous and keep pushing on anyway.

If you're going to try to learn on your own, you have to be serious about it—treat it like you're in school. Dedicate a certain amount of time every day to learning. Set deadlines for yourself. You will need the support of the other people in your life too, they have to see you as a serious student—don't let them turn you away from your goals or steal your passion.

Most students that I have taught worry about their level of talent. Almost all of them wish that they had tons of natural talent! Don't wish something like that on yourself... For many years, I've been teaching students about what I call "the curse of talent".

The Curse of Talent

The problem with having an over abundance of natural talent is that it didn't require any discipline to achieve it. Think about that carefully for a second—those people that can naturally do amazing artistic things never had to learn any techniques, theories or processes, they could just do it. Their knowledge isn't accessible to them—most of them don't know how they do what they do, nor can they teach it to anyone.

Most talented people that I have known live in fear that one day, their talent will leave them and they will be left with nothing. If they have no knowledge to back them up, they won't be able to do anything!

I know of one very famous painter that lost all of his ability when he developed a thyroid condition. If all of your ability is locked up in an inaccessible part of your brain, you're living a very risky artistic life...

I believe that the whole "you have it or you don't" attitude is a lie created by talented people to dissuade others from trying to take their jobs. You can learn anything—it just takes a lot longer and a lot more effort if you don't have much talent, but you can never unlearn what you have learned, so that knowledge will be with you forever.

You may have known someone in school that was naturally gifted with mathematics—they could add up huge sums in their heads or figure out complex equations easily. Does that mean that the rest of us are incapable of learning math? Of course not, it just means that we have to put in the effort and learn it from the ground up. Same thing with animation—you can learn it and get good at it, you just have to be willing to put in the effort and the hours and ignore anyone that tells you you can't do it.

Having no talent at all is a hardship too—it might take you a lifetime to learn what others can learn in several years, but if it's worth the struggle, you can do it. The ideal situation is to have just an average amount of talent —enough to make it possible to get great before you're old and not so much that you can skip the learning by discipline part.

There's a really good book on this topic called <u>Talent Is Overrated.</u> I'd recommend that you read it!

Essential Mental Skills

As you will hear me say many times, animation is done in your head. It is a mental discipline, not some kind of physical skill, like hockey or soccer where you need to train nerves and muscles. (I knew I'd manage to slip in hockey somehow!) Sure, if you're drawing or painting, you have some eye/hand coordination to learn but in the grand scheme of things, that's pretty minimal compared to the mountain of other things you're about to learn.

Almost all of your training is going to be mental and emotional. To smooth the path, there are some important mental skills that you must learn to make your animation training possible.

Learn to Avoid Distracting Yourself!

You probably already know a lot of the things that pull you away from your work and waste your time. TV, Facebook, e-mail, and the good ol' internet are pretty common detractors. Learn what yours are and take real steps to reduce their influence on you. You don't want to eliminate them completely, be reasonable but realistic about the time you spend with them. You still need to have a life!

I worry about people that say that "animation is their life".

No... your life is your life. If you don't live your life, you won't have any real experience to draw your performances from for your animation. Everything will be fake—an imitation of other people's lives. Living your life and having real experiences and interactions with actual living people is the best resource to draw on when you're animating. Facebook isn't real interaction...

Ignore Outside Distractions

There will always be distractions beyond your control—noisy environments, people having conversations around you etc. Instead of trying to make your environment perfect, so you can work undistracted, learn to focus past the distractions and zone in despite the environment not being perfect.

One thing that I like to do is listen to music that is emotionally related to what I'm working on. This helps me block out distractions and it can help generate visual ideas. If I'm studying, then I listen to something that makes me feel good, so I'm in the right frame of mind and emotional state to learn quickly. I tend to avoid music with words, especially if I'm reading or doing animation with dialogue—I find it very distracting, like trying to listen to two separate conversations at once.

If you have already read Richard William's book, <u>The Animator's Survival Kit</u>, then you might remember the part where he asks Milt Kahl if he likes to listen to classical music while he works. Milt's over the top response scared Richard into adopting a new mantra—Animation is Concentration. Silence worked for Milt and it worked for Richard but it's not the same for everyone. You may be like them and need perfect silence to concentrate or maybe not—experiment and figure out what works best for you as an individual.

Mental Focus

Do you know what it's like to "get into the zone"—that state where everything is flowing and the world seems to have drifted away and you're fully immersed in what you're doing? That's a feeling that you want to try to recreate every time you sit down to work or study. The problem is that it takes time to get into that zone. When you're first starting out, it could take quite a while to ramp up and get to that state of mind. Every time you let yourself get distracted or walk away for something, you'll be "out of the zone" and you'll have to start that process again.

Try to stay focused on your work or study for blocks of at least 2 hours at a time. After that, you may be a little drained, so take a break and mentally regroup, then attack the work again. As you practice this again and again, you will eventually get to the point where you can instantly get into the zone.

You will eventually get so good at focusing and holding visual information, that you will be able to stop in the middle of a complex scene, go home, come back the next day and carry on exactly where you left off without hesitation—all the important details will still be there, stored in the back of your mind.

This is a vital skill to have if you want to supervise some day. You will have to hold all the information from everyone's scenes in your head and go back and forth between them, recalling the changes you asked for, what they looked like before and what the director asked for. If you're supervising 15 or 20 animators, that's a lot of data to keep sorted out in your brain! If you can compartmentalize the data—store each scene in a different mental storage bin—then you can jump back and forth easily.

While we're on the topic of mental focus, we have to talk about a worrying trend I've seen in quite a few studios lately—Dual-tasking. I have seen far too many animators working with videos or movies playing on their desktop. Not just the audio, but an actual video screen open. You need to understand that this isn't the kind of multi-tasking that you can be good at. When people refer to multi-tasking, they are usually talking about task switching, which is very different. You switch back and forth between several tasks but you are only ever doing one thing at a time. Your brain is not capable of fully focusing on more than one thing at a time. If you ask your brain to do two things simultaneously, like animating and watching a movie, then you won't do either one successfully.

Think of it this way—if you are asked to do two things simultaneously and one of them is a reflex action or an internalized action, like riding a bike, and the other is a task that takes concentration, like reciting poetry, you will be as successful at that as you would have been at either of those tasks individually. However, if both of the tasks require concentration, like reciting poetry while writing an exam, you will not do well at either task. If you don't believe me, try writing out numbers up to 100 in 2's (2, 4, 6, 8 etc) while reciting the alphabet backwards. Both tasks take some level of concentration individually—together, they would be nearly impossible.

If you are truly concentrating on your animation, there's no way that you can have a video playing without damaging your ability to focus on your scene. How can you possibly expect to get "in the zone" when you have invited distraction right onto your desktop by having a video running? As soon as anything interesting happens in that video, it will draw your attention away from your work, forcing you to start that ramping up procedure all over again.

Another major problem with this practice is that it sets an emotional tone that is probably not in line with what you are animating.

I'm not saying that you have to eliminate watching videos altogether, I'm saying that you can't do it while you're animating. Sure, you can take a break from your scene after things start to grind, watch a video for a bit to refresh your mind and refocus, then dive back into your scene! In fact, I encourage you to do this because it prevents you from burning out or getting too jaded by your scene.

Time Management

Most people have a lot going on in their lives, but you can't let that stop you from achieving your goals. You need to find a balance in your life so you can juggle all of the important things—family, friends, hobbies, work, earning money etc. I considered not putting this section into the book because everyone knows that they need to manage their time, but when I realized that it's one of the skills that I still feel I really need to improve on, I thought I had better put it in here.

I have known people that believed that you can't have a balance—it's either all animation or all family. I have yet to meet anyone that has been happy making a decision like that. Yes, animation (learning it and doing it) will take up a big part of your life, but you can't let it take over your life completely. Make compromises to keep a balance without hurting other people or yourself in the process. There are tons of books out there on this subject—find a good one and learn well!

Manage Your Expectations

If you were to chart your progress on a graph, most people would expect it to look like a diagonal line—steady progress. Of course they would like to have it look like an upward curving line—exponential growth! However, from what I have seen time and time again, most animators progress is more like stair steps. You don't seem to be getting anywhere for a while, then all of a sudden, you make some kind of leap overnight! Then it can seem to plateau again, then another leap. On and on it goes like that. Learn to expect this and you won't be surprised or get disheartened when it happens to you.

Of course, even knowing that, some people expect those stair steps to be colossal! They expect to be Milt Kahl in a year! Here's where the "managing your expectations" part comes in...

The graph is a chart of what your actual progress is. If you drew a chart of what you _expect_ your progress to be like and compared the 2 graphs, that's where some real problems can be spotted...

Expectation vs Progress

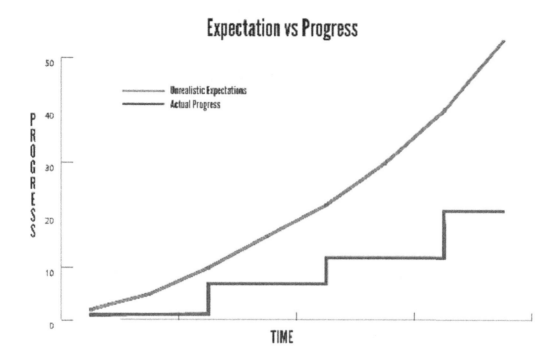

If you set your expectations way above your current level of progress, you will never be satisfied with your work. You will always feel like a failure—like you'll never make it. This kind of thinking can actually slow your progress because animation is an emotionally based job. If you are miserable, your work is going to suck—when you feel good, it flows.

If your expectations are completely in line with your progress, that's a problem too! If you don't expect more from yourself, then your progress will stagnate. It may lead you to think that you already know it all or that what you already know is good enough. No one gets great with that kind of attitude.

It's best if you set your expectations just a bit higher than your current level of ability. This way, you can set realistic short term goals for yourself to create measurable progress. Keep pushing forward but keep it real!

Critique

Remember how I said that you're not going to improve unless you get some feedback and critique from someone that knows what they're talking about? Well, it's of no use if you don't know how to take critique properly...

First of all, you need to be open to it—if you are defensive or argumentative, you have not only wasted your time but you have insulted the person giving the critique and probably ensured that they will never critique your work ever again.

Be open—listen to everything that they have to say and try to understand the point they are making and see your work through their eyes. However, (and this might surprise you) you don't have to accept everything they say and make changes based on it. Keep in mind, what I'm talking about here is when you ask someone to look at your work and give feedback. In a work situation, when your supervisor gives you a critique, you act on everything they tell you, even if you disagree with it.

When you ask for a critique, remember that the reviewer is speaking from their own subjective point of view. If what you planned didn't come through to them and their critique is based on a misconception, then it's probably because your animation didn't communicate the idea to them clearly enough, and that will have to be addressed.

If you are the type of person that gets upset by critique or finds it hard to listen to, then try to remember this:

<u>You are NOT your work!</u>

If someone is looking at your work and it's full of errors that you haven't noticed, and they start to tell you, "this is not right, this is broken, this can't move that way..." they are talking about the work, not you... They are <u>not</u> saying, "You suck, you're a terrible animator, you'll never be any good."

Yet so many people hear it that way. Instead of realizing that they have just been given the answer to how to make their shot better and not make the same mistakes in the future, they use it as a way of beating themselves up and making themselves want to quit.

Use critiques to help you see more detail in your work. You will know if something is wrong—the critique will help you identify exactly what it is and how to avoid making the same mistake again.

Learn by Doing!

Don't make the mistake of reading, watching videos, going to lectures, reading tutorials and never acting on any of it. If you don't start putting what you've learned into practice right away, that information will fade away quickly.

Think of it this way—you can spend days reading all about how to ride a bike but it doesn't make much difference until you actually get on a bike and try riding it. The reading can help prepare you for what you have to do but only when you try doing it will you be able to internalize the knowledge and really "know" how to do it. Once you know it, you can never <u>un-know</u> it. Even if you don't ride a bike again for 20 years, once you have learned it, you can pick it up again anytime. Sure, you might be a bit wobbly at first and it will feel a little strange, but you won't have to learn it all over again. Same thing with the animation skills you learn and internalize—even if you don't use those skills for many years, you will never un-know it. Sure, you'll be a bit rusty but you will get it back quickly —but only if you have internalized the knowledge by getting in there and really doing it.

Don't be ashamed of your early work. Keep all of your early tests so you can see your progress as you continue to learn. As your knowledge expands, you will see more and more detail in what is wrong with your early scenes.

As you learn from various sources, keep detailed notes—and keep them in a way that you can access them easily any time. I would highly recommend Evernote, Dropbox or Google Docs. They work on PC, Mac, tablet or phone and the notes are synced between them all, so you can access them from anywhere. Dropbox has the added advantage of keeping a local copy on your connected computers so you don't have to be connected to the internet to access your files.

Finding Critiques

If you're planning to learn on your own, where are you supposed to get useful critiques? In order for a critique to be of any use, it needs to be informed (technically accurate, from an experienced person) and impartial (it can't be from someone that is trying to please you or hurt you). With that in mind, DON'T ASK YOUR MOM! Your Mom just wants to make you feel good, so her comments would be something like, "That's very nice, dear!" That is of no use to you at all. If you are the kind of person that actually looks for that kind of validation instead of an actual critique, you need to change your focus. Stop trying to build your ego and start focusing on building your skills.

For that same reason, critiques from fellow students are of minimal use. Their work is also full of errors and they only have a very limited amount of knowledge and probably zero experience. Would you ask a first year medical student how to perform heart surgery...?

Having said that, there is still some value to student critiques. If you ask a dozen of them and they all point to the same problem, then it stands to reason that there is something there that you need to fix. They won't be able to tell you exactly what is wrong or how to fix it but they can help you spot problems.

If you're not in a school, you can still get other students' opinions online or in a peer group—you could even start your own meetup to help each other.

Don't be afraid to show your work and when you give feedback to others, remember to point out where it's not working for you but don't try to solve their problems if you don't really know the answer, you might just be leading them astray. I once listened in as a student was instructing another student to make his object fall faster to make it look heavy... I had to step in and explain Newton's second law of motion to them. (More about that in Book 2!) As helpful as he was trying to be, it would have been better for him to say "it doesn't look heavy enough" than for him to lead the animator astray and turn his mistake into a bigger problem—and worse, to teach him a "rule" that was incorrect, which may confuse him later when he is taught something opposite to that and he can't recall which information is correct!

Finding a Mentor

I know, I've said several times that you should find a mentor that knows what they are talking about but how do you do that? Why would they give up their precious time for you?

There's no easy answer to that, I'm afraid, but remember that they are just people too. They probably have a lot of things that they need or want to learn as well. Do you have skills in some other area that you could barter with?

For example, there are tons of things I'd still love to learn about or get better at, like Toon Boom, InDesign, After Effects, info graphics, painting, modelling etc. If someone offered to teach me something I wanted to learn, I'd be happy to teach them animation in return. I'm sure that there are plenty of others that would do the same. If all you are doing is asking people to give up their time to teach you out of the goodness of their heart, you won't get many takers. People's time is too valuable.

On to the Good Stuff!

So, now you know who you are, what path you want to follow and how you learn most effectively. Now, it's time to find out exactly what skills you need to learn!

CHAPTER SIX: What
Skills to Learn

This is the part that you've been waiting for! The rest of this book will lay out all of the skills you need to master to be a great animator and a plan for how to learn them.

There are 2 main categories for the skills you need—internal skills and external skills.

Internal skills allow you to visualize a scene in your head as if it was a final film or real life! Remember, animation is done in your head—most of the skills you will be learning serve one purpose: to improve your ability to visualize.

External skills allow you to get your vision out of your head and into a form that other people can see. That may be done with a computer, drawings, stop motion techniques, sand on glass or whatever. If you can visualize so amazingly well that it's like being in a different world, but your external skills are so poor that nothing can get out of your head properly, then it's all for nothing. You need to master both sets of skills to bring others into your world.

The external skills subset is much smaller than the massive group of skills I have called internal skills, as you're about to discover.

Internal Skills (In Your Head)

Here's a list of the basic internal skills you will need. Most of them are explained in detail as a book of their own in this series—they're that vast!

Visualization

Basic Principles

Physics (motion, energy and collisions)

Acting (especially improvisation)

Body Language

Physiognomy (how the face shows character)

Texture (visual dynamics, rhythm and "visual music")

Composition, Cinematography and Perspective

Anatomy and Kinesiology

Dynamic Posing

Interpreting Reference

Specialized subjects

    Animals

    Children

    Creatures

    Stylized Cartoons

    Specific studio styles i.e.. The Pixar style

I will give you a brief description of what these skills entail, then, in the next chapter, I will teach you how to learn them!

Visualization

As I have mentioned, visualization will always be your primary skill—it's what makes you an animator. Most of the other skills you learn serve to improve your ability to visualize.

Think of your visualization skill like a muscle, (an old cliche, I know, but it's very appropriate) it will only improve with regular training and if you don't use it, it starts to diminish.

This is a skill set we should all have been developing since we were children. Every time a child turns the world around them into something else, whether it be playing with dolls, running around with a stick or acting out their favourite characters, they are building their ability to visualize.

Unfortunately, that kind of imaginative play has been disappearing for the past several years. I have seen it happen with my own children and it worries me greatly! Kids today have too much served up for them and they haven't needed to imagine things for themselves. Kids walk around with cell phones and media devices now, watching a steady stream of content from the internet as well as the usual suspects, tv and videos, being used as babysitters instead of as entertainment.

I used to see kids playing together, becoming a character, like a superhero or a character from a movie and improvising in character with their friends. More recently, it seems to have shifted to kids reenacting what they have seen in a video—that's using memory, not imagination... or worse, there are a lot less kids that go out and play at all! It gets harder and harder to get kids to even go outside or play with toys since they would rather be gaming or watching videos of some kind.

Here's the real problem—watching all this entertainment does NOT improve their imagination or ability to visualize new things. Yes, it improves their visual memory but that's not the same thing at all.

As I said, I saw this happen with my own children and this is how it came to my attention. I have always loved reading to my kids at night. It started with picture books for young children and progressed to books with less and less pictures until we eventually moved on to complex, picture-less books, like Harry Potter and Lord of the Rings.

Eventually, they all got too old to want me to read to them but I saw an interesting pattern. My eldest son liked hearing stories for quite a long time, then went on to become an avid reader. My second son stopped wanting the stories at an earlier age and didn't really read many books himself afterward. My third son lost interest in stories as soon as we moved to books with no pictures and he had little to no interest in reading on his own (until he was much older). When I asked my third son why he had lost interest, he said it was because it was hard for him to figure out what was going on without pictures.

I asked them all what their visualization was like when I was reading to them. My eldest said that he felt immersed in the world—he could see everything around him in full colour and detail. For my second son, it was more like watching a movie—detailed but not immersive. For my third son, it was more like symbols that represented things, like a symbol for a castle or a simple picture of a horse, etc.

I realized that their ability to visualize was in direct proportion to the amount of imaginative play that they had when growing up. The more they played, the better their visualization.

When my fourth son came along, I made sure that he had a healthy balance of imaginative play mixed in with the other forms of entertainment and sure enough, he has an excellent ability to visualize and absolutely loves stories being read to him. We even moved on to picture-less books much earlier than I did with the other boys.

It's never too late—start now. Daydream, read books, play with your children if you have any. Spend time every day seeing things in your mind —not memories, but things that you haven't seen before. If that's too hard at first, try imagining things or places that you know well but imagine what they look like from an angle or direction that you're not used to seeing them from. What does your house look like from the top? (No fair using google maps...)

(Time for a shameless plug)

This discovery led me to start creating a series of children's books that were designed to build the reader's imagination and ability to visualize. Designed for tablet devices and smart phones, they have a high quality fantasy painting and a short clip of full feature quality animation with sound and music to give the reader all the information they need to be able to visualize what is happening in that setting. The animation only covers one action on the page, the rest is up to the reader to visualize, but they will already know how the characters and settings look, what they sound like and what their movement and body language is like. Each page is a new setting, with a new image and animation. This should act as a crutch for the reader to help guide them through the visualization process.

At the start of each book, the reader can choose their age level and the story will be served up in one of 3 age-appropriate levels from preschool to young adult. The text and narration will be in multiple languages to make it accessible to as many people as possible.

My goal with this is to help train young people to use their imagination and strengthen their visualization. As they get stronger, they will get more and more out of books without pictures and will hopefully learn to love reading. There's nothing more empowering for a child than a love of reading!

Basic Principles

Disney's Nine Old Men compiled a list of principles (not rules) that were consistently helpful in their style of animation and in many other styles too. If you're an Archaeologist type, then you probably see these as the only rules of animation. Pioneers will see this as a great foundation but not the end.

They were originally printed in the book <u>The Illusion of Life</u> and have been reprinted and explained (sometimes incorrectly) on countless websites and in other publications. I won't explain them all here, just do a google search for "The 12 principles of Animation" and you can read all about them there. The purpose of this book is to explain the things that you can't find elsewhere.

Having said that, in book 10 of my series, I will be covering the 12 principles with examples so you can learn them in the context of a scene, plus I will list and describe some of the other principles that I have encountered, such as <u>storypoint</u> and <u>leading the audience's eye</u>.

These principles, the old and the new, are tools that you will use every day, but not necessarily all of them will be appropriate to every scene. Most of the errors you make in your early work will be due to the fact that you forgot or disregarded a basic principle.

Physics

This is one of my favourite topics in animation and one that I love to teach! Most of the basic principles of animation are subsets of two overriding concepts—<u>physics</u> and <u>texture</u>.

Squash and Stretch, Follow Through and Overlapping Action, Slow In and Slow Out and Arcs are all direct results of physics. You will often hear someone critique your scene by saying, "The character doesn't have enough weight, add more squash and stretch". Your first reaction to that will probably be, "That's great, but how much?" The way to know how much or how little is to understand the laws of motion that are in effect in every single scene that you animate.

Book 2 in this series is completely dedicated to physics for animators and it will cover Newton's 3 laws of motion as well as other important topics, such as types of energy and how they are transferred (specifically related to animation) collisions and much more. Don't be too frightened—there won't be any equations or concepts beyond what you will use every day in your work.

If you want to get a head start, there are several good websites out there that will give you a good grounding in basic physics. I highly recommend that you check them out, but note that most of them aren't specific to animation, so there might be more info than you need. There are links in the Education section of this book.

Acting

All animators have to be able to act—there's no avoiding it. However, acting for animation is very different than stage or screen acting, so don't think that you have to go to acting classes or spend any time on a stage. If you already have acting skills, they will help you immensely but there are still aspects to animation acting that you will need to learn to succeed.

Book 3 will cover acting for animation in depth but if you'd prefer to get a head start, check out the book Acting For Animators by Ed Hooks. There's a link in the Education section.

Body Language

Everything that a character does with their body has to show what they are thinking and feeling (both emotionally and physically). However, it's very rare that both the face and the body are telling the same story... The face shows what your character wants to project to others, while the body tells what the character is really feeling, for the most part.

I will cover all of this in book 5 and a bit deeper in book 17.

Physiognomy

Yeah, I know it's a strange term but it is the assessment of a person's character or personality by their physical features, especially the face. This is the primary concern of character designers but as an animator, you have to be very aware of the expressions and postures that make an audience understand clearly the depth of your character's personality. Also, you have to understand how those habitual expressions and postures alter a person's face, form and general posture. If you are consistent with how you handle a character's physiognomy, the audience will be able to instantly read the specific personality of your character without them having to do or say anything.

In book 17, I will cover these concepts but more importantly, I will teach you how to study people and build a mental library of character traits to create characters that are easy to read and identify with.

Texture

As I mentioned earlier, texture is an overriding concept that many of the 12 principles of animation stem from.

Anticipation, Staging, Straight Ahead and Pose to Pose, Secondary Action, Timing, Exaggeration and Appeal are all derivative of texture.

Unfortunately, the concept of texture seems to have been mostly forgotten. Book 6 is dedicated to this wide ranging concept. If you are a musician, a dancer, or if you have studied music theory at all, you have an advantage! Many of the concepts of texture, such as the creation and resolution of tension, directly relate to music theory. I will show you how texture is essentially, the "visual music" in animation. It's the difference between having a character that moves around and one that seems to have a life of its own and has strong appeal.

Composition, Cinematography and Perspective

If you've done any drawing or painting, you're probably fairly knowledgeable in the concepts of composition, but that is the 2d composition of still images... composition for animation is a bit different because it happens (and changes) over time, so for lack of a better term, it's like 4d composition. It's an aspect of cinematography, so in book 9, I will cover composition for animation as well as some basic cinematography and perspective.

Anatomy and Kinesiology

Even if you are only interested in stylized cartoon characters, you still need a basic understanding of anatomy or you won't know how to caricature it. You need to understand how people are structured and also, any animals or creatures that you plan on animating. The more realistic the animation, like in visual effects, the more important a solid understanding of anatomy is.

Kinesiology is the study of how joints move. So, just like composition, it's not enough to understand anatomy, you have to understand how that anatomy changes as a character moves. You also have to understand how all of the joints and muscles function so you can animate believable motions.

For example, I can't count the number of times I've seen animators turn a character's head to the side past the shoulder... sure, you can do that, but no one would survive it unless they were an owl... If you don't know the limitations and the planes of movement, then you always run the risk of animating something physically impossible that doesn't look like an exaggeration of reality, it just looks flat-out wrong.

Dynamic Posing

Although this is really part of texture and body language, I think you need to think of dynamic posing separately.

If you've already been animating or have had some training, then you've probably already had it drilled into your head that you need to have <u>strong poses</u> or your revision notes said to <u>work the poses</u> or worse, you were given some term that makes no sense at all, like <u>commit to your poses</u>.

That's all great but what exactly is a strong pose and how do you achieve that? It's not enough to simply copy poses that you have seen in films or drawings or even from reference footage that you have shot yourself.

Dynamic posing isn't just poses that are extreme or pushed really far, it's more about the energy they contain. If you think of the famous sculpture of David by Michelangelo or The Thinker by Rodin, you will begin to understand that it is the feeling of life and energy in the pose that makes it dynamic, not how big or stretched out it is, or even how straight the line of action is.

After you learn about physics and you understand the concept of potential energy, you will be ready to learn how it all can be applied to create really dynamic poses.

Again, poses for animation are not exactly like poses for drawings, paintings or sculpture. Those art forms have the pose locked in a single moment of time. You will often be taught that you should be able to read everything about a character's action and intent in a single pose. That is true, however, that pose doesn't happen in any one single frame, it plays out over a short span of time... There's no better way to make your animation look stiff and fake than to have every body part hit the extreme of their pose all in one frame.

Book 7 covers this concept as well as body language.

Interpreting Reference

Gathering and shooting reference is the best way to get all the subtleties of action and character into your scenes. However, there are some specific techniques for how you turn that footage into animation and it's not simply copying it verbatim. It's more like the visual equivalent of writing a book summary—taking the most important elements and distilling them down into a form that is concise and simplified.

Book 8 covers how to shoot reference properly, how to interpret it and even how to deal with motion capture, which is becoming a necessary skill to have in today's industry, even in cartoon styled films!

Specialized Subjects

Even after you have mastered all of the skills we have talked about so far, you're probably still going to have a small panic attack the first time you have to animate a 4 legged animal, especially if they are doing something complex and your deadline is tight... I have dedicated a group of books (from 11 to 16) to specialized subjects and I will continue to add to that list over time on my website.

External Skills (With Your Hands)

The list of external skills is quite a bit smaller but each topic is complex and involved. These are the methods you have available to get your animation out of your head and into a medium that other people can experience.

Computer Skills

Software

Drawing for Animation

Specific Tools of the Trade

Computer Skills

Before you spend a lot of time learning specific software, you should take to time to learn the basics of how computers work and the ins and outs of the operating systems you might have to use. It's not good enough to be a "Mac user" or "PC user" exclusively anymore. This hit me like a bolt of lightning the day I started on District 9 at Image Engine, when I discovered that they were running Linux on their systems and I had never touched it before... I felt like a fool not even being able to get Maya opened...

My lead, Jeremy Mesana, taught me what I needed to know to get by in a few hours. It only took a couple of weeks to get comfortable with it but I could have saved myself (and Jeremy) a lot of trouble if I had taken the time to learn the basics earlier with a few simple Google searches.

The other important thing is that you don't want to be completely dependent on IT to fix every little problem you run into, like accidentally hitting the Shift Lock key... Learn how computers work so you can figure out some of the issues that go wrong all by yourself. This will be especially important if you decide to freelance and you don't have an IT department to back you up.

Since there are about 8 kajillion websites, courses, magazines and books about computer skills and operating systems, I won't be covering it at all in my series.

Software

When I moved from traditional animation to 3d, I found learning the software to be a shock to the system and very taxing! That was 1999... today, most software is a lot more user friendly and easier to jump in and start using. Like I said before, you're not going to be able to learn everything, so limit what you study to just what you need to know. If you're going to be animating in Maya, you don't have to learn the modeling tools or anything to do with texturing or cloth—just learn the animation tools and other basics, like making a playblast (a movie file of your work in progress.) After you have mastered the animation tools and workflow for all of the software packages that you'll need to use in various studios, you can venture into acquiring other complimentary skills. It's good to have a few extra skills on the side to keep yourself employed when animation work is scarce. However, I would be cautious about announcing your extra skills to your employers for reasons that I will cover later in the pitfalls section.

After animating exclusively in 3D for several years, it took me a long time to go back to 2D animation because everything had shifted over from drawings on paper to using software like Toon Boom, Flash or TVPaint and I didn't have a clue how to use them. If you want to stay versatile and keep yourself gainfully employed, learn to use the most popular 2d and 3d programs—namely, Toon Boom Harmony and Autodesk Maya.

There are untold resources for learning Maya and a good few for learning Toon Boom as well. Now, with OpenToonz as a free and powerful 2d animation tool on the market (the software that Studio Ghibli uses!) I can see it taking a large share of the 2d market—you should learn that one too!

In book 18, I will cover the basic concepts of various types of software but I won't go into all the details of what buttons to push—that's what those user manuals and websites are for. Instead, I will teach you how to use the software to actually animate and I will cover some workflows and best practices. Most of the examples will be the methods that I use myself and what I have observed from other people. In the future, I will have video interviews on my website with other animators that will show their personal workflows and methods learned in various studios. Look for them at www.HowToAnimate.net.

Everyone has their own favourite way of working, so it's worthwhile asking as many people as you can what their workflow is and what extra tools they like to use. There are plenty of third party tools and plugins out there (many of them free) that will make your job a bit easier.

Many of the big studios use their own proprietary software but don't worry —they all function in the same basic way, so if you learn one, you're well on your way to understanding them all.

Drawing for Animation

Even if you are only interested in 3D animation, I would highly recommend that you spend some time learning to draw. I don't mean that you have to become a master draftsman—you just need to learn how to get your poses and ideas out of your head quickly and accurately. If you can draw rough thumbnail images that represent what's in your head in an appealing way, then that's enough.

If your goal is to do 2D or traditional animation, then you will obviously have to spend a lot more time studying drawing! Drawing and animating are two separate but very closely related skills. I was taught that animation is the <u>language</u> and drawing is the <u>vocabulary.</u> If your vocabulary is limited, you're not going to be able to communicate your ideas to your audience very well.

You can be the best draftsman in the world without knowing the slightest thing about animation but it would be very difficult to become the best animator in the world if you're completely incapable of drawing.

Drawing is too big a topic to cover in these books but I may gather some friends and create a book in the future that will show you many different styles and methods of drawing.

Specific Tools of the Trade

If you're planning to do stop motion animation or some other medium, like chalk on walls, sand on glass etc. Then you will have to learn the specific tools and techniques of that format. However, it's nearly impossible to get away from computers nowadays, so even if you're going to have a career in stop motion, you're probably still going to have to have computer skills if you want to work for a studio.

CHAPTER SEVEN: How to Learn These Skills

So, now you know what internal and external skills you need to master. How do you actually go about acquiring all of these skills?!? It may seem pretty daunting but if you have a good plan, you can learn it all quickly and retain it forever.

These are the 4 main components of your training regime. I call them the 4 Pillars of Learning Animation. This is the process you will use for the rest of your life to keep improving your skills.

> **Education** - Websites, blogs, tutorials, books and subscription sites, like Pluralsight.com and Lynda.com
>
> **Observation** - Studying life and the world around you.
>
> **Analysis** - Studying other people's animation and breaking down reference.
>
> **Practice** - Internalizing the information by actually doing it yourself.

Education

If your plan is to teach yourself, then you're going to need a lot of good resources. You can and should do Google searches to find new and interesting sources of information but you don't want to plan your whole education around a "cross your fingers and cast a line" approach.

I have gathered a lot of books, blogs, websites and videos over the years. I'll add links to the reference section of my website and update it as often as possible. I have a short list at the end of this chapter to start you on your way. If you have a list of your own that you would like to share, please send it to me at chris@HowToAnimate.net and I'll check it out. If I think it's a good addition, I'll add it to the reference section and give you credit for the find!

If you ask for recommendations from your friends, beware of the "bandwagon mentality". Many people will recommend a book or training course because they heard it was good or simply because it's popular. If they haven't actually used it themselves, chances are, their recommendation doesn't really mean a lot.

Whenever you find a great resource, write a review or a blog post about it. Send it out on Twitter or Facebook—let people know! We need the best resources to be easier to find, so you can help make that a reality.

Yes, but Is It Animation?

Don't assume that just because a book or course is called "character animation" that it will teach you how to animate. There are actually very few books out there that will teach you how to animate. Many that I have seen are about how to use software (just restating what's in the manual) or what buttons you push in an animation program to accomplish things. Some of them have a section on animation but that tends to only take up a few pages and is a reiteration of the 12 principles or maybe just a couple of principles, like squash and stretch. The rest of those kind of books is usually taken up with things like modeling, rigging, storyboarding etc.— Everything except actual animation...

My point is, once you've learned those basic principles, you don't want to keep reading the same thing over and over again. What you need is fresh information—ideas and techniques that are different than what you have already learned.

The same is true for many schools that I have seen—the curriculum is designed to teach you software and other external skills but there isn't much focus on the all-important internal skills. Of course, the schools that are dedicated to animation, like Animation Mentor, iAnimate or Animschool are the exception to this.

Everything Relates...

If your ambition is to do cartoony styled animation, you might think that you don't have to learn things like anatomy and physics but trust me, your cartoon work will be far better if you have a solid grounding in reality first. Cartoons caricature and exaggerate reality—how can you caricature something that you don't understand? You'll have to understand the rules before you can decide which rules can be broken and which can only be bent.

Yes, you can do whatever you want in a cartoon but that doesn't mean that everything looks good... If you do something that is just clearly wrong for no reason, it will just look bad. If you break rules of anatomy for no reason, like having a character's hand on backwards, it's going to look wrong.

If you're creating a cartoony superhero and you simply invent nonsensical muscles, it will look like bad, childish artwork. Sure, you can simplify musculature or even add muscles that don't exist in reality, as long as they make some kind of logical sense—an exaggeration of real muscular structure.

I will teach you lots of methods for doing this in subsequent books (like book 13—Animating Invented creatures) but my point for right now is simply to let you know that you will have to learn the basic skills that are relevant to all styles of animation, especially anatomy, physics, drawing and composition.

Blogs and Forums

Yes, blogs and forums can be a great resource for getting information and learning new skills but what really makes them great is that they are interactive! Go ahead, ask your favourite book a question and listen to the stony silence...

If you find a great blog, written by someone masterful, or a forum that is filled with informed people that post regularly, get involved and ask a question, or lots of questions, and you will not only get answered, you will also be building your all-important network! Who knows, you may even find yourself an awesome mentor that way! Just don't forget that you have to contribute too—answer people's questions if you're able. It's important to give and take.

Don't be afraid—every author, blogger and forum poster is just a person, like you. At worst, they could ignore your question completely but you might also get a piece of advice that changes your career and your life! Or, you may develop a friendship that lasts, who knows unless you try.

I have friends that I worked with for years that I met in forums—some of them I never met in real life! I've gotten freelance jobs simply by posting in forums before. It's more powerful than you may realize!

Let me tell you a little bit about one of my favourite living artists—James Gurney. He's the creator of the popular Dinotopia series of illustrated books that eventually was developed into a tv series. He's been an illustrator for decades and even worked in animation as a background painter.

He is also the author of several fantastic books—none of which are about animation but he is a phenomenal teacher! He has a world class blog that he posts to regularly and he even does a ton of high quality video blog posts and training videos.

So why am I talking about him over any of the great animation bloggers out there? Well, because he's someone I was genuinely scared to contact.

What if he ignored me or just shut me down or turned out to be really unfriendly? It only mattered because I admire the guy so much! But I took the risk and contacted him after I finished reading <u>Imaginative Realism</u> and <u>Color and Light</u>. He responded back right away and it started a long e-mail conversation. I had some specific questions I wanted to ask him but I didn't ask them right away—that would be a little disrespectful. Before I asked him to give up some of his knowledge, I tried to find a way to give him something of value first. I told him how much I enjoyed his books and offered to help spread the word about them as far as I could. Hopefully, that has resulted in more awareness and more sales for him. Look, I'm doing it again right now...

He answered my questions happily. If I had just jumped in and asked him to give me some gold without even offering to do something for him, he may not have been as forthcoming.

I know from my own experiences that you react differently to "takers" than you do to "givers". I've had people email me out of the blue, asking me to critique their work or to answer a Skype call and teach them things. When I was younger, I would often have people ask me to draw them something or animate something for them. To make it worse, they would devalue what I did by saying something like, "It will only take you a few minutes" or "I'll give you twenty bucks, what's the problem?"

They weren't offering to do anything for me or to teach me anything, so it really didn't motivate me to spend my time on them.

There were other times when someone would lend me a hand with something or do something nice for me and I would repay them with a drawing. I was happy to do so because I felt that they deserved it.

Try to keep that attitude when you approach an author, blogger or potential mentor. Ask yourself what you can do to help them and genuinely do it for their benefit—not just so you can get something from them. Be respectful, be kind and be generous and you never know—maybe years down the road, the favour will be returned.

Same thing in forums—if you're going to post comments, do it respectfully and genuinely try to help other people, don't just barge in and try to ask a million questions.

Resources

Here's a short list of resources—check my website for a more in depth list. www.HowToAnimate.net

Software Training

I've always preferred to be shown how to do something than to simply read about it, which is why I preferred buying dvd training courses instead of books. (I still bought a ton of books, though...) Recently, some of the best training companies have moved to the online subscription model and you will save a ton of money that way!

Here are my 4 favourite sites. You don't need to sign up for all 4 of these examples—they are all a little different in their approach and content.

www.pluralsight.com (formally Digital Tutors) Pluralsight has a vast library of all sorts of topics and they tend to be handled very well!

www.lynda.com - Their videos tend to be good overviews on a variety of topics.

www.thegnomonworkshop.com - Gnomon handle technical aspects of 3D very well at a granular level. They also have training courses in painting and other art forms.

www.3dbuzz.com - I personally learned my initial 3d skills at 3DBuzz. It won't teach you how to animate, but neither will any of the other sites I just listed either. What I really loved about 3DBuzz is the way that Jason Busby explained the "why" behind everything! It gave me a solid understanding of how 3d works and I'll never forget it.

Websites

www.animationphysics.com - A series of great videos from Alejandro Luis Garcia on physics for animators. They cover a lot of the same things that I cover in book 2, so why am I promoting him when it sounds like we're in direct competition? Because we're both giving away our information for free, so why not?

www.donbluthanimation.com - Don Bluth's own website—with tutorials and training videos.

www.animatorisland.com - One of those rare websites that actually gives animation advice!

www.bloopanimation.com - This site has grown recently—it has a blog, tutorials and now, full courses you can get for a decent price.

creatureartteacher.com - Aaron Blaise is a former Disney animator—his website has a bunch of high quality lessons on animation, drawing and painting for a very good price!

www.kennyroy.com - Kenny and I were mentors together at Animation Mentor. He and I both started creating our own video lectures for our students to add to the curriculum. Kenny is carrying on that tradition on his website. You have to sign up and log in to get to the good stuff.

Forums

www.11secondclub.com - The 11 second club hosts a monthly contest plus a very active forum—a great place to go for critiques and inspiration!

www.awn.com/forum - A great big, world renowned animation forum! Go have some fun!

www.animatedbuzz.com - The forum is a bit small but they have a sort of Tumblr-Like section for uploading animation and portfolios that is pretty cool.

animationforum.net/forums/index.php - A forum that seems to have more beginners than some of the others but a good place to build connections.

Blogs

CartoonBrew.com - This is more of an animation news website and blog but it's huge and always relevant.

www.garyfaigin.com/faigin-face-blog - Gary Faigin is a master of expressions! His book "The Artist's Complete Guide to Facial Expression" has been one of my most used and necessary resources for most of my career. He started a blog recently that you should visit frequently.... And go buy that book too!

splinedoctors.com - One of the most informative blogs and podcasts out there!

livlily.blogspot.ca - A fantastic source of traditional animation pencil tests to learn from!!!

www.speakingofanimation.com - A blog and podcast, lots of great info!

www.gagneint.com - Michel Gagne is an old friend and an amazing animator—he's been blogging since 2001, so you have some catching up to do.

Books

The Animator's Survival Kit - Still one of the best books out there for helping you get started in animation.

The Illusion of Life - Written by two of Disney's "Nine Old Men", It's a very big book but well worth reading. It mixes instruction and insight with lots of stories of life in the early days of the Disney studio.

The Artist's Complete Guide To Facial Expression - I mentioned Gary Faigin's blog—this is his masterful book! As I said—every animator used this book when I was in traditional animation. I don't see it as much any more, but I should...

Observation

In this chapter, I will help you to understand how you need to change the way you see the world around you—to start thinking like an artist and like an animator.

If you come from a very left-brained background and you're used to thinking very logically, analytically and mathematically, then you're going to really have to stretch yourself to start using that right hemisphere to develop your imagination and visualization skills. Then, you will be able to use those analytical abilities in harmony with your imagination to extract the most important elements from the things you see.

Unlearning

First, you have to train yourself to stop seeing things as symbols and see them for what they really are. Sounds kind of vague, doesn't it... Think of it this way—if I asked someone to draw an eye and they had very little drawing skill, the first thing that they would probably do is think of a universally recognizable symbol for an eye.

Yep, it's an eye. Everyone would understand that it is meant to be an eye. However, it's not <u>my</u> eye or <u>your</u> eye or even the eye of anyone you know. No one in the world has an eye that looks exactly like that.

Symbols are completely generic. They are the complete opposite of a specific representation. If I handed you a photograph of your own eye and I asked you to draw every single line and every bit of shading that you see in the photo, then what you create will represent <u>specifically</u> your own eye— not mine, not your mom's.

Now, consider how many people do exactly the same thing when they are visualizing things, especially things that they have never actually seen before in real life, like a castle, for example. Unless their ability to visualize was highly developed, they will tend to reach for generalizations —a symbol for a castle.

We all do this to some extent, even if you have a good imagination. If you were walking down the street and you saw someone get into a car and drive away, you might remember what the person looked like if you were focusing your attention on them, but would you remember the specific details of the car? Probably not—you might remember the colour, the general shape and maybe the brand and model but would you remember the licence plate number, the exact shape of the fenders? The image in the reflection on the hood...? Of course not, unless you're blessed with a photographic memory. But... If you were specifically looking for those kind of details, there's a good chance that you will be able to remember details like that in the future when you have to design a car...

Make it your goal to look at the world in a new way—to always be looking for the specific details of the things you observe. It's not possible to take in every detail of everything you see every day, of course, but if you walk out of your door this morning and say to yourself,

"Whenever I see a bird today, I'm going to look at the shape and colour of its beak. I'm going to compare the beaks of all the different birds I see."

Then you will have started to develop your mental "bag of tricks" for your own visual library. Make this your new way of seeing the world.

Don't try to take on too much at one time, especially in the early days of studying. If you are going for a walk down a busy street, don't try to analyze people's walks, just focus on one aspect of their walk, like how they place their feet or the timing of their hands when they swing their arms. Look at that one detail on everyone you see and compare them. What makes each person different from the rest? How does the timing or nature of that movement make you feel about that person? Does it give you some insight into their personality?

Learning from Life

In the analysis section, we will talk about how you break down reference from videos but remember that it's not enough to just watch videos to really understand the nature of something.

Anyone that has seen something truly breathtaking in real life, like a volcano, a great white shark or the curve of the Earth from the edge of space would tell you that it is a much richer experience than simply watching a video of the same thing.

If you want to be able to breathe life into your animation, you have to get out there and actually live! You can't spend all of your time behind a desk, trying to imitate life if you have no idea what it feels like to actually do the things your character is supposed to be experiencing.

If you want your character's performance and action to be truly convincing, you have to know what they're going through—how it feels physically and emotionally to be in their situation.

Let this be one of your new mantras—If you can't feel it, you can't animate it.

That doesn't mean that you have to have lived through absolutely every kind of experience in the world—you just have to have dealt with something comparable. For example, you don't have to climb Everest to know what it feels like to accomplish something exceptionally hard. If you've ever faced something scary and out of your comfort zone, like sky diving, indoor rock climbing or even climbing a tall ladder (especially if you're afraid of heights) then you will know very well how it feels to accomplish something like that. If it's a relatable experience, it's enough to be able to get that feeling into your animation.

Tunnel Vision

Don't be discouraged if you're having a hard time seeing the details in things you observe or if you have trouble remembering the details later. If you work at it every day, you will continue to get better at it. When you're first starting out, it's like you have tunnel vision—you can only see and comprehend a very narrow range of things or one thing at a time. As your artistic abilities improve, you will be able to understand and absorb a lot more of what you are seeing. One day, you will realize that you're seeing the whole world in a way you've never experienced it before!

The more you learn about art and animation, the more you will see in the world around you. Just wait until you start learning about physics and composition—that will change everything for you!

Plotting Movement

When I was very young, I remember being in the playground in my preschool, watching a little girl riding a swing. As she moved back and forth, I could see the arc of her movement like it was a ribbon of light in the air. I didn't realize it at the time, but that was probably the one natural ability that I had that predestined me to become an animator.

As I got older, I could track multiple objects at once and see them form a pattern, like rhythmic gymnastics or streak photography. I could watch someone running and track the motion of their hips, head, hands and feet all at once. When I talked to people about it, I realized that not everyone could do it. It made me feel kind of special and it was fun, so I did it all the time. Little did I know that that was exactly the kind of deliberate practice that allows you to master a skill!

When I became a traditional animator, I saw people doing that very same thing right in their shots by putting down a separate piece of paper and placing dots where the centre of mass was on every key, then drawing a line through all of the points—it's called tracking arcs. When I taught that technique to animation students, I understood that this was a skill (like many others) that can be learned by anyone, not just an ability that you either have or don't have.

Start looking for these patterns of movement all around you. Start simple, like following the path of birds. Try to really visualize the path, like they were leaving a trail behind them, like the light cycles from TRON. When it starts to feel natural, work your way up to more complex things or groups of objects. If you want to get really complex, watch the patterns of wind on tall grass or water!

Recognizing Composition

Book 9 in this series is all about composition—it's way too complex to tackle it here (that's why it has its own book...) but let me touch on one important aspect of it now, so you can start paying attention to it as you're out observing the world.

You may already have some knowledge of pictorial composition as it pertains to paintings and drawings but those rules are designed for still 2 dimensional images. Even sculpture, which follows 3 dimensional rules isn't enough. Animation happens over a period of time and the observer's point of view changes over time, so it's more like 4 dimensional composition!

A better term would be Cinematic Composition, which is essentially, the rules of composition over time and with a moving perspective. There are some very good books, videos and courses on cinematography—Here are a few links—check my website for more!

Hollywood Camera Work - www.hollywoodcamerawork.com

Elements of Cinematography - www.elementsofcinema.com/cinematography/composition.html

Elements of Cinema - www.elementsofcinema.com/cinematography/elements_of_cinematography.html

Patterns of Behaviour

There's an exercise in Book 3 (Acting) that I'd like to bring to your attention now so you can get used to practicing it. It will get you into people watching in an organized and constructive way.

Go someplace where you can watch people that don't know they're being observed, like a park or a coffee shop. Pick someone that catches your attention and immediately guess what that person is like. Try to figure out their personality, what they are feeling and thinking. It doesn't matter if you are right or not, what matters is the immediate first impression that you get.

Then, start asking yourself questions—what is it about the way that they are sitting, moving or holding themselves that made me come to that conclusion? What was my first clue? What gave me the strongest impression? Is there a pattern to the style of movements they make that reinforces my impression?

This exercise is the exact reverse of the process you go through when you are handed a scene to animate. The director will tell you what the personality of the character is and what they are thinking and feeling. It's up to you to figure out how that character should move and pose so the audience gets all of that information about the character in an instant—the same way that you did when you watched people in the coffee shop.

The more people you study, the more you will build your own mental library of patterns of behaviour that clearly show specific character.

We will go much deeper into this in book 3. Until then, get practicing!

Analysis

When I started learning animation, there was no such thing as the internet, so my education came from the few books on the subject that I could find, some ill-conceived observation of the world around me (no one had taught me how to study or what I should be looking for) and a whole lot of practice. My greatest tool, though, was analyzing video.

My parents had just bought an amazing Sony betamax machine that allowed me to go single frame forward and in reverse. Sure, go ahead and laugh but this was a miracle at the time! It allowed me to go frame by frame through animated and live action movies and study the nuances that I couldn't catch watching at full speed.

I was blown away when I saw how much exaggeration there was in certain frames and how big the spacing was between drawings when an action had to happen quickly. I couldn't see any of these things when I played the videos at normal speed. I remember stopping on certain frames in Pinocchio and The Secret of NIMH and being flabbergasted at how stretched out or how squashed the characters were and that it was absolutely not visible at full speed, even when I knew it was there and was looking for it!

I remember having that same feeling the first time I saw ultra slow motion video shot on a Phantom camera. When you see something like a water balloon bursting at 25,000 frames per second, it feels like you've just entered a secret world, full of things that you've never seen before.

As mind blowing as this was to me as a teenager, I didn't benefit from the videos as much as I could have if I had known what I was looking for. I was just feeling my way through the dark, trying to figure stuff out on my own.

The experience would have been very different for me if I had been learning about animation, then using the video analysis as "lab work" for my studies. That's what I encourage you to do and it's why analysis is the third part of your four part study system.

When you learn about a principle or aspect of animation, like say squash and stretch for example, then you look for examples of it in the real world, then you can look at animated videos and see how other people used squash and stretch in their work to interpret and caricature reality.

You may be tempted to just study how the great masters of animation did it all and mimic their work. The problem with that is that your work would be a copy of someone else's interpretations of reality. If you don't understand the subject you're animating; if you don't understand acting or composition or physics; then your work will be an obvious hack job.

It's like seeing a wannabe comic book artist that draws lots of semi-logical lumps and bumps that are supposed to be muscles. Anyone that has a half decent understanding of anatomy (or has ever seen a few muscular people before) will see that the "artist" created muscles that don't make sense, connection points in the wrong place, muscles overlapping the wrong way (or blending together into a shapeless mush) or those cool old symbols for muscles, like the tic-tac-toe six-pack... Even viewers that don't know anything about anatomy will see that the drawing is completely wrong— they just won't know why...

You need to learn the principles and techniques, then study how master animators have used those principles in their work and see what you can take away from that to use in your own work. The key is, that you have to <u>understand</u> what it is that you're borrowing from them.

How to Analyze Video Reference

Book 8 is all about how to use reference effectively but for now, I'll give you a quick introduction to studying reference material.

First, you will need a way of watching videos in slow motion forward and in reverse. DVD's and Blu-Rays aren't great for that because they are compressed, so going in reverse tends to skip a bunch of frames—you want to be able to see every single frame! It would be best if you could watch them on a computer and use a good video player that gives you an easy way to go frame by frame. My 3 favourites are GOM Player, QuickTime 7 and RV. If you know of a better one, let me know!

There's also an awesome app called Coach's Eye that allows you to scrub through video and draw over top of it to! What a perfect analysis tool!

You can find almost any kind of reference you want on YouTube but their built in player doesn't allow you to go frame by frame. If you're using Firefox, there's an extension you can get called Video Download Helper that will allow you to download YouTube videos to your computer so you can play them in one of the video players that I mentioned. (Just make sure that it's not illegal to do that in your country...)

Keep in mind that live action and animation follow different rules, so you will study them for different things. When you're watching an animated video, study the following things:

- Try to see the arcs

- Look at how much they've exaggerated the poses and action

- Look at the timing (how many frames did they use to create each action?)

- Pay attention to the spacing (how big or small is the change between each frame?)

- What did they do to make you look in a particular place at a certain time? (Did they lead your eye on a deliberate path?)

- How have they placed the characters and the camera (staging) to make the scene interesting to look at?

- Can you see how the poses and placement of the characters, the setting and lighting create the composition—good or bad?

- What are the rules of the style they are using? What kind of things do they do all the time and what can they not do?

If you're watching a live action video that is preplanned and uses actors, then you will study it for different things than a documentary or candid video. Just like studying people in a cafe, you should pick one aspect to study at a time. Perhaps in one session, you chose to study how a character's personality can be defined just from the way that they walk. Choose films that have very distinctive characters—like The Big Lebowski or Léon: The Professional. Another time, you could choose to study how they stage the characters and how their placement and poses lead the audience's eye wherever the director chose. One of the best examples I can think of is Young Frankenstein—every scene is a study in staging, composition and leading the audience's eye!

Once I find a really good film for reference, I tend to go back to it again and again. There are some that I have used as examples in my teaching for many years. I'll provide you with a short list here and tell you what you should study from them. I will make a much more comprehensive list on my website in the reference section.

If you're trying to figure out complicated body mechanics or a difficult action that you're not familiar with, then any kind of video will do as long as it's shot decently. If you need to study how a horse changes gait from a trot to a canter or if you need to have two characters fighting with two unique styles of martial arts and it needs to be accurate, then you absolutely need to use reference—not to copy, but to gain an understanding of how it all works. There are also plenty of things that we take for granted that may actually be very different than we assumed them to be—like the way a helicopter or light plane flies, or the way a dog sticks its butt out to the side to walk. Of course, if you don't understand an action, it's best to learn a bit about it before you start trying to study it on video—you need to know what you're looking at. A few google searches might be all you need!

Candid video of people is excellent for seeing true emotion as long as the person being filmed is unaware of the camera. Films aren't as good for studying emotion, since everyone is acting... Of course, you wouldn't want to study a candid video for its staging, since there isn't any. Choose what you want to study, then choose the appropriate type of video for the job.

Sometimes, the reference that you need the most simply doesn't exist, so you will have to shoot your own. I will cover that in depth in book 8 as well as techniques for breaking down and analyzing what you see. It will also cover how to shoot, edit and interpret video for helping you act out your shots. I'm also planning some video blog posts to demonstrate it all visually.

Every time you find a good piece of reference, keep it for future use. You may need access to your reference when you're away from your own computer, so I recommend storing it in a structured folder on an online service of some kind, like Dropbox, Evernote, Amazon Drive, Google Drive, or any other system that you can use from any computer anywhere.

Movie List

Young Frankenstein

Leon: The Professional

The 5000 Fingers of Doctor T

Across the Universe

The Secret of Nimh

Pinocchio

How to Train Your Dragon

Practice

As I mentioned earlier, it's not enough to just read a bunch of books or watch dozens of tutorials or training videos. Unless you put that knowledge into practice and use it to change how you see the world, then all that you have learned will quickly be lost.

Deliberate Practice—Every Day!

I want this to be your first and most important goal on your road to success in this industry. Seriously, the only way that you can fail at this is to skimp on practicing or to do it without a plan.

I know this for a fact because I regularly screwed it up...

I have spent years reading books about drawing and painting and I read countless books on software and 3d when I was trying to transition from traditional animation to 3d animation. I got a lot of information from it all but precious little knowledge. Why? Because I was always too $&€£ing afraid to put it into practice!!!

All those books and videos are just tools for learning. It's like a big literary screwdriver. A screwdriver doesn't tighten or loosen a screw—you do! You can hold a screwdriver and stare at a screw for years and nothing will happen! You have to <u>use</u> the tool to get a result.

Sure, it sounds like a silly analogy but it's true. I spent years reading books and watching videos and it did very little to make me a better artist. Yes, my life was (and still is) very busy and yours probably is too but if you can't fit in time to practice, there's no point wasting your time reading and learning if it's all going to fade away.

I beg you not to waste your time like I did. Don't wait until New Year's Eve or when the time is "just right" or the planets align... Make a resolution today to practice (even a little) every day.

Years ago, I found a guy on the internet that was determined to become a painter. His work was absolutely terrible but he vowed to practice every day and he posted his efforts every single day to prove it. If you skip from the beginning to 1 year later, the change is remarkable!!! Every day, he got imperceptibly better—sometimes a little worse, sometimes he made little leaps. He kept it up and he achieved his goal, just like you will—one day at a time.

Keep and Use a Sketchbook.

You've probably heard people ask this question before, "If you could go back in time and give some advice to your younger self, what would it be?"

For me, the answer would be, keep and use a sketchbook every day! It's not that I never got that advice from others, it's that I never followed the advice because I didn't want to draw attention to myself—I didn't want people to look at my work and judge me when my drawings looked like crap.

You may be expecting me to say something like "don't be afraid" or "don't worry about what other people think" but that's not realistic. If you're afraid, you're afraid—you can't just stop being afraid because you choose to. Hell, I'm still afraid to let people see my work unless it's a finished piece. Your sketchbook is supposed to be about experimentation and practice, not a showpiece to be paraded around.

So here's my advice (if you're like me)—draw every day in your sketchbook, but don't tell anyone you have it and don't show it to people. Let it be your safe place to experiment, develop and screw up. This is for you and your own development.

The last thing you want to do is start limiting yourself to drawing what you already do well, so you don't show weakness to people that will be looking at your sketchbook. You need to be free to make lots of bad drawings—you need to work on your weaknesses, not hide them.

With that in mind, I want you to agree to something right now. You need to give yourself permission to suck. That's right, your work will probably suck for a very long time. Even when you think what you've done is pretty cool, if you look back on it in 10 years time, after you've gotten much more knowledgable, you're going to see how badly it sucks. And really, that's ok! That's how everyone learns!

Don Bluth said something to me once that I will never forget. He said that for every good drawing in you, there are ten thousand bad drawings. You have to get through those ten thousand bad drawings to get to the good one. The more you practice, the smaller that ratio becomes. Keep practicing and you might get it down to one hundred bad drawings for every good drawing. You might not live long enough to get to the point where every drawing is good, but you only lower the ratio with practice. Ok, I'm paraphrasing, but that was the gist of it. (It was over 25 years ago...)

Practicing Other Skills

Ok, that's sketching and drawing out of the way, but what about animation and acting and computer skills and all those other things on the list of internal and external skills?

Like I said before, when you learn something new, put it into practice immediately. It's the only way to really <u>internalize</u> the knowledge. Remember my analogy about learning how to ride a bike? You use the information that you gathered to make your practice purposeful and not just random experimentation. Once you get the hang of it, you will really know it—you have absorbed it and internalized that knowledge. Once you know something in that way, you can never forget it.

It really is that simple—learn how to do something and practice what you've learned until you have internalized it and you don't have to think about it anymore.

It seems pretty obvious how you would apply this to some of the technical aspects of animation—if you're learning some new software, try doing some experimental animation in that software. When you get stuck, read more about it. But... how do you apply this to the more abstract things like physics...?

Since physics is such a huge part of animation, it's not something you can just do a few exercises with, then say you've got it. You have to learn how physics <u>feels</u>—as yourself and as the characters and objects that you animate.

Here's where the "riding a bike" analogy is really relevant!

Practicing Physics

There is a ton of information to learn about physics—you have to use that knowledge to make sense out of the forces you see and feel every day. For example, there are a bunch of standard exercises that animation students do in school, some of them are physics exercises but they often aren't presented that way.

"Lifting a heavy object" is one that you see in every school or online course. However, if you don't learn the physics behind it and learn the way that people deal with physics in the back of their mind as they perform tasks like this, then all you will be doing is mimicking the look of the example you're given.

I know, this still doesn't make a lot of sense—but let me run through this exercise from two different mindsets and it might make more sense.

Scenario 1 - The animation student (let's call him Justin Otheranimator) is given an assignment that involves having a character step up to a heavy box, then lift it up. The teacher demonstrates the action and has an animated example to show him how it should look. Justin uses his visual memory to recall what the teacher looked like doing the action and he watches the example frame by frame and tries to copy what he sees. He doesn't think about physics, he just tries to make it look like the example. The teacher looks at his poor imitation and says, "It doesn't look heavy enough. Make it heavier."

Poor Justin is at a loss... How do you make it look heavier? He tries using some techniques he has seen other people use—he stretches the characters arms, he makes his expression more strained, he even adds some shaking to his arms. Something is still wrong—it's getting overworked, yet it still doesn't look heavy—he just looks like a bad mime... Even if the teacher holds his hand and tells him exactly what to change, it will only fix this one shot. As soon as Justin tries to animate something heavy again, he will make all of the same mistakes because he doesn't understand the physics behind it.

Scenario 2 - When Justin is given his "lifting a heavy object" assignment, he recalls the basic Newtonian physics he learned in high school. He remembers that all objects have a centre of gravity—the point of balance.

He remembers the law of inertia—all objects that are still tend to stay still and an object in motion will stay in motion, in the same direction and the same speed forever until another force acts on it.

He thinks about the heavy object and how it's going to resist being moved. He thinks about his character and how he has a centre of gravity (COG) of his own. He knows that as soon as the character grabs the object, their two masses become one, with a new centre of gravity between them. He recalls that people will only use as much energy as is necessary to perform a task, so his character won't use all of his strength to lift the object—he will only use as much as is needed to lift it.

Before he starts to animate, he does some experiments to understand how the action feels and what is really happening with the physics. He sets up a video camera to study the action later. Then he grabs an empty box and pretends it's heavy. He immediately feels foolish for making such an obvious mistake... If the box is light, then how is he going to feel the true physics of lifting a heavy object? He finds a sandbag and tries again. Now it feels right! He goes through the action again and again. Step up, bend down, grab the bag, stand up.

Later when he's reviewing the footage, he notices something very interesting—the way that he lifts the bag changed from the first test to the last. He compares just the first and last and tries to figure out why they look different. He finally spots it! The first time he tried it, he took longer at the point where he grabbed the bag and began to lift. He also noticed that he did a little bit of resettling of his feet and hands before he was ready to lift. In the last take, he simply planted his feet, grabbed the bag and lifted...

The difference, he realized, was that he didn't really know how heavy the bag was at first or where exactly the COG was. By the end, he knew it very well. In order to lift the bag with the least amount of force, he had to get his own COG as close to being directly above the COG of the bag as possible. The further his COG was from the bag's, the harder it would be to lift. As soon as his hands touched the bag, he could feel tiny vibrations that let him know that the bag was solid and it was heavy. He wouldn't know exactly how heavy until he started to lift, but based on this initial bit of info, he made adjustments with the placement of his feet to get in line with the bag's cog. As soon as he started to lift, he could tell <u>exactly</u> where the bag's COG was and how much force he had to apply to lift it.

He decided that the character he was animating shouldn't know how heavy the object was, so he decided to put those little foot and hand adjustments into his shot. Then, when the character started to lift, he would have him move his hips in closer to the object because it turned out to be heavier than he expected.

(Of course, the teacher used Justin's shot as an example to the class, then secretly hated him for doing a better job of it than his own example animation...)

Do you see where I'm going with this? As you are learning the principles of animation, you need to start looking for examples in your daily life and experiment to get to know what physics feels like in your own body. For example, if you're in a car and the driver is a little heavy on the brake, feel how everything in the car, including your own body, wants to keep going forward at exactly the same speed (and same direction) until another force acts on you. In this case, the seatbelt stops you from continuing to move at your current speed. Also, once the car has fully stopped, why do you still feel like you're being pulled forward and why is the chassis of the car leaning forward for a second, then suddenly bumps down and stops? After you learn about inertia and the transference of energy, it will all make sense. You will also be able to use that knowledge to predict what will happen in many situations.

If you go hiking up a steep hill or walking up a flight of stairs, pay attention to what happens when you plant your foot down. Where is your centre of gravity? How have you moved it to be able to take that step?

Where are you applying force? Which muscles are being used and how are they making your body move up and forward?

Once you get a better understanding of how it all works in your own body and in objects you can see and feel, you'll be ready to start imagining beyond that. How would it feel to be a baby crawling up some stairs? What if your head was 10 times bigger than it is now? How would that change the way that you move to keep your COG in the right place when you walk up the stairs with that giant noggin?

Practicing Acting

You may already know that a lot of animators go to life drawing classes to do gesture drawing. Those quick, loose 30 second sketches help you in many ways but is there a similar method for improve your acting? Of course there is—it's called Improv (improvisational theatre). You may have heard of improv and thought it was only for comedy sketches but that's not true at all—it's actually a training method for actors that usually involves the group of actors (or the audience) coming up with a setting, a character (or occupation) and an action or goal. Then the actors have to immediately get into character and start performing, taking cues from each other and rolling with the bizarre changes as the story develops and morphs.

You can see the obvious parallel with animation—this is exactly what you do when you animate a scene—you're given a character, a setting and a situation and it's your job to immediately get into character and create a rich performance. Unlike a live action actor, you may have to switch characters several times in the one scene and play characters that are not physically possible for an actor to play, so you had better be good at switching characters and being able to develop real depth of personality instantly. Improv will help you develop that.

Animation Exercises

You will probably want to spend the bulk of your time practicing actual animation, and why not! Just be sure to follow a plan for deliberate practice—you don't want to keep doing the same kind of thing over and over again, avoiding your weaknesses and ignoring the principles you're supposed to be learning.

If this is the early days of animation for you, then keep in mind that your exercises are practice pieces, not show pieces! They don't have to entertain an audience, (unless that's what you're practising) they are just meant to help you drill the fundamentals into your brain and make them second nature. You will never ever put any of these experiments onto a demo reel. (No, seriously. Don't... ever.)

What Software?

If you're doing 3d animation and it's your first time, you're going to have to choose some software to use and find a free rig to do your tests with. Thankfully, you can get trial versions of the big expensive programs and some of the smaller ones can still be great to learn with and are relatively cheap.

Maya is the industry standard. If your plan is to work in the VFX or cartoon animation industry, then this is the program to learn. Most of the biggest companies use their own dedicated software but learning Maya will help anyway because all professional software is pretty similar.

Softimage XSI is also awesome but unfortunately it has been absorbed into the Autodesk juggernaut and is now discontinued.

If you want to use less expensive software for your own personal work, the three best I know of are Poser, Daz Studio and Hash Animation:Master. Many people swear by Blender, which is powerful and free, but since I've never personally used it, I am reluctant to recommend it. You can always check it out for yourself, it's free, so why not?

Poser and Daz studio are very similar—they are both powerful consumer programs and come with built in libraries of characters and animation. They also have a vast (and I mean VAST) community of third party developers constantly creating new content that can be used in both Poser and Daz Studio. The only problem is, since it's a very different way of working than Maya, it won't help you get a job. Daz Studio is free—hard to say no to free, right?

Hash:Animation Master is super cheap and very powerful. You can do everything in it, just like Maya and the workflow is similar to Maya too, so it would be a good starting point to get into the industry.

Maya - http://www.autodesk.ca/en/products/maya/free-trial

Poser - http://my.smithmicro.com/poser-11.html

Daz Studio - https://www.daz3d.com/get_studio

Hash Animation: Master - http://www.hash.com/home-1-en

Blender - https://www.blender.org

If you're going to do 2d, then you can use OpenToonz for free! (The same software that Studio Ghibli uses!) Alternatively, you could get a trial version of Toon Boom Harmony. Personally, I'd recommend OpenToonz if you plan to learn one software and stick with it to do your own projects but if you want to work in the kids tv industry, you'd better learn Harmony. Some places still use Flash (now named Adobe Animate CC) for certain shows but those days are numbered.

OpenToonz - https://opentoonz.github.io/e/

Toon Boom - https://www.toonboom.com/products/harmony/try

Adobe Animate CC -
http://www.adobe.com/ca/products/animate.html

A Word of Warning

Do not, I repeat DO NOT try to make a short film right away...

When you know what you are doing, sure—go for it, but when you're just starting out, it's a huge mistake.

You will hear me say this a lot in these books and in live classes and lectures. From what I have seen, it's like artistic suicide if you don't know what you're doing. Sure, it's great to hear your young son or daughter playing in a music concert when they've only had a few weeks of instruction on an instrument. You will be so proud of them as they honk and squeak their way through the most elementary tunes imaginable. But imagine if you went to see a concert of adults that sounded like this and you had to pay to get in... Now imagine that you're a solo performer in front of a large audience—all of whom are expecting brilliance, and there's you, barely knowing how to even hold your instrument properly...

Is this really how you want to present yourself to the world? Beyond that, you are opening yourself up to a world of pain as you encounter every obstacle and difficulty imaginable as you slog your way through. You may actually finish it, it may actually look good and maybe, just maybe, it won't cost you a fortune to do it but the odds are against you and if your goal was to learn how to animate, then you've done it backwards—a short film should be a graduation piece, not the beginning of your training.

Sorry if this sounds overly negative but I've seen too many people get completely discouraged by biting off more than they can chew. Also, they use up a lot of the time they had set aside to study, doing all the various parts of making a short film that have nothing to do with actually animating. All that time that they spend lighting, rendering, painting and compositing would be better spent improving their animation skills.

What I would highly recommend that you do at the beginning of your training is to animate a series of short experiments. Focus on one theme, principle or problem and practise it lots of different ways until you really get it, then try another and another.

This is what most animation courses focus on—lots of exercises like turning 180 degrees, stepping up on a box, opening a door, jumping, lifting a heavy object etc.

The problem I have with many of the school curriculums that I've seen is that the students often animate these tests only once and without a solid understanding of why they are doing it. How many people that animate a character lifting a heavy object are like scenario 2 of my example of Justin Otheranimator? Not as many as there are like scenario 1—the ones that don't know what they are supposed to be learning from the exercise...

Walks and Runs

Another thing I take issue with is the way that character walks and runs are treated like basic beginner exercises. Walks are really hard!!! Sure, you can follow along with an example of the basic 8 frame Preston Blair walk cycle but that's like the animation equivalent of drawing a symbol for an eye... You should be able to tell everything about the personality of a character from their walk. There are millions of ways of varying the components of a walk to show individual character—you can't just plug the Preston Blair walk into any character and expect it to look good. If I was preparing the curriculum for a school, I would leave walks and runs until much, much later in the learning process. It's a delicate dance of complex physics, body mechanics and acting—not for the uninitiated!

Clichés and Symbols

Even though I just said that you should animate one small experiment at a time, that doesn't mean that you should reach for obvious clichés or turn your animation into a generic symbol for an action or emotion. You should still imagine that whatever character you're animating, even if it's a simple flour sack, has a specific personality and he or she will do the action in their own particular way. This is where the improvising comes in.

For example, if you're animating a flour sack stepping up onto a small box, ask yourself:

> How tall is it?
>
> How much does it weigh?
>
> How old is it?
>
> What gender?
>
> Do they have an occupation?
>
> What kind of temperament?
>
> do they have any physical issues?

Keep asking yourself questions and coming up with immediate, improvised answers until you really get a sense for who this character is, then you'll know how they should move. Your test may not necessarily convey their personality as clearly as you would like but that's why you're practicing... Someday, it will be clear to everyone.

As an example, if your character was a 5 year old boy that was climbing up on the box after already being tired out from playing and running around, he would climb up on that box in a very different way than a middle aged female neurosurgeon stepping up to a podium to accept an award.

Be specific and your animation will never look clichéd. Make sense?

Getting Some Feedback

As I mentioned early on, the biggest advantage of going to school over learning on your own is feedback. You need to have good feedback and constructive critique from informed sources. Having said that, it can actually be difficult to find that in many schools...

When you're learning on your own, the wisest idea is to post your work on forums and ask for critiques. Make sure you pick a forum that has a lot of experienced animators and artists. Anyone can tell you if they like your work or not but people with some experience can point out what is wrong with your work. Artists with a lot of experience can tell you what is working and what is not and, more importantly, they can teach you the principles behind what you did right and wrong, so you can repeat your successes and avoid making the same mistakes.

As with any new skill that you try to acquire, you shouldn't try to be everything at once. First, get the basics down, then try to get good at it, then you can worry about getting fast. You won't be able to do it all at once.

Blank Page Syndrome

If you are trying to learn 3d animation, you may already have a computer that's ready for action and a trial version of Maya open and ready to go. But then, you stare at that empty viewport with just a grid sitting in the middle of it and you ask yourself, "Now what the hell do I do...?"

Do not be tempted to start learning how to model and rig a character—that will be a handy skill in the future but right now, it would just delay your progress. What you need, is a ready-made rig that you can just load up and start using!

There are some pretty sweet free rigs out there now that you can easily download and use. I've listed a few here but keep an eye on my website for more. I'll put up links whenever I find a good one—or perhaps I'll have a talented rigger make some for you to use... "Hey Paxton! I've got a job for you!"

Mery - http://www.meryproject.com/

Morpheus - http://journal.joshburton.com/2010_08_01_archive.html

Animation Mentor - http://www.animationmentor.com/free-maya-rig/

Malcolm - http://animschool.com/DownloadOffer.aspx

Ball rig - https://www.bloopanimation.com/best-free-maya-rigs/

Four Sack - https://coffeetd.wordpress.com/2013/04/17/free-rig-flour-sack-2013/

Dragon and more - http://www.cgmeetup.net/home/downloads/free-maya-rigs/

Horse rig - http://www.mothman-td.com/portfolio_items/horse_rig/

Practise What You Learn

Remember to learn internal skills at the same time as external skills and use them to compliment each other. For example, as you learn about physics, do short animated exercises that demonstrate one principle of physics. As you learn about composition, do some sketches to test out different ways of staging and posing characters that lead the viewer's eye, following the compositional rules that you just learned.

Learn; look at the world with an artist's eye; study references and keep practising!

Oh, and DON'T MAKE A SHORT FILM! ...Yet!

CHAPTER EIGHT:
Avoiding the Pitfalls

It would be naive to think that your road to animation greatness is going to be smooth and easy. Even if you have a great plan, a perfect attitude, all the time and space you need and endless willpower, there will still be many obstacles along the way. Some of them are predictable—let's go through a few of those and how you can overcome them. I will be the first to admit that I have fallen into most of these traps myself over the years, that's why you can trust me when I say that these obstacles are surmountable.

Chapter 1 Syndrome

This is an easy trap to fall into when you're in your early years of animation and learning rapidly. As you learn and improve, you will start to see the flaws in work that used to look wonderful to you and you will know how to improve it. That's a great thing—the problem is that you might be tempted to go back and revise your own work endlessly. The term "chapter 1 syndrome" comes from the writing world but it's exactly the same problem. When a writer keeps going back to rewrite a chapter because they know they can improve it, they will never finish their book.

Likewise, if you keep going back and revising your old work, you will be narrowing your focus. It's far better to take what you have learned from your mistakes and use that to make your next scene better.

I really fell deeply into this trap in my early years—even when I couldn't go back and revise, I always felt the desire to, like unfinished business hanging over my head.

I remember when Disney released The Little Mermaid—I was working on Rock A Doodle at the time and I had recently finished a scene with The

Duke and all of his owl cohorts in the song "Never Let Him Crow". After seeing how much detail and attention was put into the "Kiss The Girl" sequence in The Little Mermaid, I felt that I could have put more into my own shots. Don Bluth was my directing animator at the time, so I showed my pencil tests to him every day. When I told him that I wanted to go back and revise my shots, he must have immediately realized I was falling into that trap. He grabbed me by the shoulders, looked straight into my eyes and said forcefully, "Never look back!!!" Use what you've learned from those scenes to make your next scenes better but never look back!"

As I read through this manuscript, I realize that a lot of my old stories and life lessons seem to have come from Don Bluth... He's a great teacher and mentor and it was an important stage of my development. I wonder where I would be today if I hadn't found a mentor like him to steer me on the right path...

The Ego Roadblock

Yes, this is a competitive business, like many, but it isn't cutthroat. You don't have to fight and scramble to claw your way to the top. You get there by being good at what you do. If you want a leadership role, like a supervisor or director, then you have to be good at leadership—being a great artist isn't enough.

Some people fall into the trap of bragging and self promoting to convince other people (and perhaps themselves) that they are better than others and deserve promotion. There is almost no advantage to doing this and tons of disadvantages.

For example, shamelessly self promoting will make you look like a jerk to everyone and even if you do rise to a position of authority, who's going to want to work with you? Beyond that, it's also terrible for your development. Remember in the section about managing your expectations,

I warned about the danger of thinking that you know it all—you will stagnate and stop improving.

Even if you don't act outwardly egotistical but you allow yourself to think that way, you will stagnate. You need to accept the fact that you will be learning for your entire life—you will never know it all. Accept that and learn to love being a perpetual student and you will continue to thrive. As life coach Tony Robbins puts it, "You need to stay green and growing".

The Downward Spiral

This is an emotionally based job—when you're feeling good, everything works well and your work just flows! When you're down, your work starts to suck pretty badly. So, it seems obvious that you need to try and stay up, right? Yeah, but when your work starts to suck, it's easy to get worried that it's going to stay that way or that you'll get worse, which gets you more down—which makes your work worse, which depresses you further, which... well, you get the point.

So what do you do when you get caught in this whirlpool of bad feeling...? Remember way back at the beginning of this book when I got you to figure out what it was about animation that you're passionate about? Well, this is one of the uses for that knowledge. Your passion is your anchor—it will be your reason to carry on when everything starts to go grey. Simply ask yourself why you got into this business in the first place—what makes you go on? Sometimes, just recalling why you got into this business is enough to kickstart your passion and keep you going.

Emotional triggers are another great trick. Have you ever been in an animation studio and looked around at animators desks that are filled with toys, memorabilia, pictures, figurines, posters etc? It's not because animators are just big children—well... that's not the only reason... Those are emotional triggers that keep you in your "happy place". If there's a movie that was really inspiring to you and you have a bit of memorabilia at

91

your desk, just looking at it can trigger those same feelings that you had when you watched the movie.

Losing Your Focus

It can be easy to lose sight of things sometimes—you can forget what the story point was in a shot and end up focusing on the wrong things. You could lose perspective in your career in general or in your balance between work and your life or family. I learned a great trick from some great animators that really helps keep you focused—simply making yourself a small sign and putting it right in your line of sight, like at the top of your monitor.

The first time I ever saw this was when I shared a room with the great T. Dan Hofstedt. One day I saw a sign on his desk, pasted at eye level that simply said "Make the most of your 8 hour day!" I've used that one a few times myself—it has prevented me from falling into an overtime mentality —pacing myself for a long day when there was really no need to be working excessive overtime. It also helped when I needed to maximize my time at home without sacrificing my work.

I've seen people use signs to remind them of basic principles, like "squash and stretch" if that's something they tend to overlook; signs to remind them of the correct process, like "broad strokes, then details" to help them break bad habits and many others.

Two of my favourites that have saved my butt are "Make it shittier" and "I'm not an accountant!" The first helped me blast though a giant stack of tv work when I kept getting caught up in irrelevant details and kept falling into a feature mindset. My apologies to accountants out there, but for me, that would be one of the worst jobs I could imagine having. Normally, I love my work, but I've been in some jobs that threatened to eat my soul— that little sign helped me survive them!

It's the Mileage, Not the Hours

The number of years you've been in the industry mean very little compared to the mileage you've put in. Remember, it takes roughly 10,000 hours of hard work to master something. That doesn't mean that you can sit on your butt for 9,999 hours and expect to be a genius after your next hour of work. You need to be consistently working at learning and improving your skills.

Likewise, doing the same thing day in, day out for 10,000 hours will not make you a master of all forms of animation. You will be damn good at the one thing that you have been doing but if you don't ever expand your horizons, then your knowledge will be limited to a very narrow path.

Don't get me wrong, I'm not saying that you should spend lots of time learning completely different skills, like rigging or compositing but if there are complimentary skills or other styles of animation that you want to learn, then you need to incorporate them into your training schedule.

The other problem with branching out to skills like rigging is that if you tell anyone that you have that skill, you might get stuck doing rigging on a film that you would have preferred to have been animating on... I've seen it happen.

So what do I mean by complimentary skills? I'm talking about things that directly enhance your ability to animate well, like acting, sculpture, martial arts or music, to name a few. How does music relate? Just wait until you read Book 6 - Texture and you will be very surprised!

Refreshing Your Palate

Overwork is just as destructive to your progress as getting distracted! If you try to work for too long a stretch without a break, you run the risk of becoming desensitized to what you're seeing and your work will start to suffer.

You know what it's like when you stare at one colour for too long—your eyes become desensitized to that colour and it starts to turn grey. You have to look away or close your eyes for a while to be able to see that colour again. Also, with taste, if you eat too much of the same thing, you lose your ability to taste it properly and you have to refresh your palate to taste properly again.

If you try to focus on your animation for too long a stretch, you start losing the ability to tell if it's working or not. If you keep trying to press on, you run the risk of making the scene worse and worse without realizing it. In order to recharge your brain, you have two options—step away from your work or have a second scene going that you can switch to.

Switching scenes will keep you productive for longer but even that has its limits. There's only so long you can remain stuck in your work before your brain starts to shut down and you start getting snow-blind.

Don't Neglect Your Personal Development

It should be pretty clear by now that in order to excel in animation, it's not enough to just develop your skills, you also have to work on your confidence, problem solving skills, time management and other life skills. There are a gazillion books, videos and courses on personal development—take your pick. If you are looking for a suggestion, I learned a ton from Personal Power II by Tony Robbins.

CHAPTER NINE: Getting
a Job

If you're brand new to animation, then you've got a lot of learning to do before you try to land your first job, but I thought it would be worthwhile having a chapter about it so you can plan ahead. If you've already got some experience and you're looking for advice on how to make the job-hunting process easier, then this will help too.

Do Your Homework

Do you remember the animation mindset spectrum I mentioned? Next time you're looking for a job, research the companies that you're interested in to try to determine where they lie on the spectrum. Are they in line with your own mindset? If not, then think twice about applying there. Sure, there are plenty of times that you will take any job going and you really can't be that choosy about your first jobs, but if you're looking for a long term job that you will actually enjoy, make sure that it suits your alignment.

Check out the company's website to see what they are currently working on and the type of projects they've done in the past. If it's a service studio, taking on jobs from clients, rather than producing their own IP (intellectual property), then the jobs they will be doing in the future will probably be very similar to what they've done in the past. The chances that they will be doing something radically different than what's in their studio demo reel are pretty slim unless they are a true pioneering studio and the work on their reel is incredibly diverse.

Demo Reel Do's and Dont's

When you find a studio that you're interested in, ask yourself what you can show them that will prove to them that you can do the kind of work that they do, without copying their work. The rule is, you don't show lightsabers to ILM and you don't show Mickey Mouse to Disney... Sure, it's tempting to show them that you can work in their style but think about it—they do that kind of work day in, day out. If you show them something that they already know like the back of their hand, all they will see is flaws because they know that stuff way better than you do, guaranteed—and it would be very arrogant of you to think that you can do their work better than they can...

Far better to show them something impressive that <u>relates</u> to what they do, that isn't a copy. You could send an alien creature test to ILM or a disney styled character to Disney as long as it is <u>not</u> a character from any of their movies.

With that in mind, the best plan is not to try to make a "one size fits all" demo reel. It's far better to re-edit your demo reel to make it specific to the places that you are sending it to. If your reel is made up mostly of productions that you've worked on, then don't be tempted to fill the reel with everything that you've ever worked on... Add and remove shots based on what the company that you're sending it to is looking for <u>right now.</u>

For example, if the company that you really want to work for does a lot of creature work but they're currently working on a giant robot movie, then your reel should lead with giant robot animation—even if it's just one test that you made specifically for them. After that, you can show creature work to prove that you will be useful to them in the long term.

My point is, from the employer's perspective, it doesn't matter how amazingly talented you are—if you can't do what they need right now, then you are not the right candidate for them. The world's best cartoon animator would not be useful to a company that is doing realistic superheroes with motion capture...

If you're looking for your first job, don't put student work or exercises on your demo reel—there's nothing that will brand you more as having no experience than having student work on your reel. It makes you look desperate. It would be far better to animate one or two shots specifically for the kind of company you're trying to get hired by and let that be your entire reel.

The golden rule of demo reels is "show no weakness". If you have 10 shots to put on your reel and 5 of them are great, 3 are pretty good and 2 of them are not very good at all, then my advice is to only use the 5 great shots and leave the rest out. It's far better to have an incredibly short reel that is full of strong shots than a reel that is longer but a mixed bag of quality. They will remember the weakest shots and that is the impression they will have of you. They may also worry that you don't realize that those shots are weak—that's a red flag! If you can't tell if your work is good or bad, you'll be almost impossible to train.

I have hired people off of one shot before. In fact, many of the decision makers in animation studios don't look too much further than the first couple of shots before they decide if you are worth hiring. If they have a good eye, they will be able to tell everything they need to know about your abilities from even one shot.

Short and Sweet

There's a lot of advice out there about how to make a great demo reel and not all of them say the same things. There are plenty of people that recommend putting your best scene first and your second best scene last, so you leave them with a good feeling about you. However, you can't be sure what the last shot they see will be—what if they don't watch the whole reel? Many recruiters don't—they haven't got the time to watch all the way through dozens of reels a day. My advice is to put your best shot first and make sure that it relates to what they are working on. Follow that with your second best shot and any work that relates to other types of work that company does or plans to do. You want to show that you have diversity and will be useful to them for years to come.

The only time you would want to have a long reel is if you are trying to find freelance work and you are putting your reel out for people to discover —you will need to demonstrate every kind of style that you can handle well, you are essentially fishing for any kind of work you can get and the companies will be coming to you to see if you're suitable.

Usually, you would only apply to a company if they are advertising that they need animators but don't be afraid to send your reel and resume to companies that aren't looking for people—they probably won't hire you but you will be on their radar and if they like what they see in you, then they will put you in their files and might call on you in the future when a position that you would be suitable for becomes available.

I haven't planned on writing a book specifically on making a demo reel and getting a job but I will pass on everything I know on my blog in the future.

CHAPTER TEN:
Summing It Up

If you've read through the whole book (and forgotten half of it) then use this summary to refresh your memory.

If your plan is to avoid going to an established school and teach yourself how to animate, here's the path:

1. Learn who you are

What is it about animation that you're passionate about?

What is your place on the Animation Spectrum? An Archaeologist, a Pioneer or somewhere in-between?

Set some goals: make a 1, 5, 10 and 20 year plan.

2. Learn how to learn

Figure out how you learn best: books, videos, audio, dabbling or all the above

Set deadlines for yourself and treat it like school

Defeat your personal doubts and win the mental game!

Learn what distracts you and how to avoid it

Learn how to focus and get into "the zone"

Get good at time management (you're going to need it!)

Manage your expectations—it's going to take a long time to get good.

Keep your ego in check or you will stop learning

Learn how to take critique—"you are not your work"

Learn by doing—start practising what you learn straight away.

Keep your tests to check your progress

Find a mentor

Barter with other people—trade knowledge

3. The skills you need to learn

Internal Skills

Visualization

Basic principles

Physics (motion, energy and collisions)

Acting (especially improvisation)

Body Language

Physiognomy (how the face shows character)

Texture (visual dynamics, rhythm and "visual music")

Composition, Cinematography and Perspective

Anatomy and Kinesiology

Dynamic Posing

Interpreting Reference

Specialist subjects

    Animals

    Children

    Creatures

    Stylized Cartoons

    Specific studio styles i.e.. The Pixar style

External Skills

Computer Skills

Software

Drawing for Animation

Specific Tools of the Trade

4. The 4 main components of your training regime

Education - Websites, blogs, tutorials, books and subscription sites, like Pluralsight.com and Lynda.com

Observation - Studying life and the world around you.

Analysis - Studying other people's animation and breaking down reference.

Practice - Internalizing the information by actually doing it yourself.

5. Avoiding the pitfalls

Chapter 1 Syndrome - never look back. Learn from your mistakes to make the next piece better.

The Ego Roadblock - don't be arrogant, even internally or you will close many doors.

The Downward Spiral - This is an emotionally based job—use triggers to keep yourself up.

Losing Your Focus - Leave yourself notes to keep on track and don't get distracted by other things.

Milage Vs Hours - 10,000 hours of deliberate practice.

Don't Neglect Your Personal Development - You need to develop your life skills as well as your artistic skills.

6. Getting a Job

Use what you know about your place on the spectrum to find the right job for you.

Research each company before you apply.

Make a demo reel that is relevant to the company's needs at the time.

Keep your reel short and sweet—show no weakness.

Never be afraid to apply—they may need you someday if not today.

Made in United States
Orlando, FL
03 January 2025

56758776R00070